easy crochet
Weekend

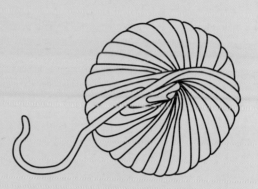

easy crochet
Weekend

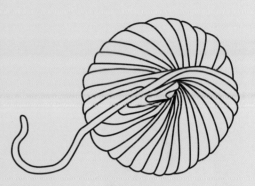

30 quick projects to make for your home and to wear

Consultant: Nikki Trench

hamlyn

An Hachette UK Company
www.hachette.co.uk

First published in Great Britain in 2013 by
Hamlyn, a division of Octopus Publishing Group Ltd
Endeavour House
189 Shaftesbury Avenue
London
WC2H 8JY
www.octopusbooks.co.uk

ISBN 978-0-600-62837-8

A CIP catalogue record for this book is available from the
British Library

Printed and bound in China

10 9 8 7 6 5 4 3 2

Contents

Introduction

Crochet is easy, and it grows fast. Master a few basic stitches (and the terminology) and you can create stylish crocheted items to wear, use to decorate your home and as gifts for friends and family in next to no time and with minimal experience.

Whether you are a relative beginner, a confident convert or a long-term aficionado, there are projects here to delight. While your first attempts may be a bit uneven, a little practice and experimentation will ensure you soon improve. None of the projects in this book is beyond the scope of even those fairly new to the hobby. Even the most basic of stitches can be translated into covetable items.

It is immensely satisfying to create something from scratch, and even more so when this is achieved in a short space of time. All the projects in this book, which range from stylish items you can wear – hats, scarves and slippers – through to practical accessories and trinkets such as a laptop bag and gift charms, can be completed over a weekend. All would make charming, unique gifts.

Crochet essentials
All you really need to get crocheting is a hook and some yarn. For many projects that's it, and where additional items are required, most of these can be found in a fairly basic sewing kit. All measurements are given in metric and imperial. Choose which to work in and stick with it since conversions may not be exact in all instances.
- **Hooks** These are sized in mm (with 'old UK' sizes given as well) and can be made from wood, plastic, aluminium, bamboo or steel. The material affects the weight and 'feel' of the hook, and which you choose is largely down to personal preference.
- **Yarns** Specific yarns are given for each project, but if you want to make substitutions, full details of the yarn's composition and the ball lengths are given so that you can choose alternatives, either from the

wide range of online sources, or from your local supplier, many of whom have very knowledgeable staff. Do keep any leftover yarns (not forgetting the ball bands, since these contain vital information) to use for future projects.
- **Additional items** Some of the projects require making up and finishing, and need further materials and equipment, such as needles (both ordinary and round-pointed tapestry ones) and thread, buttons, ribbons and other accessories. These are detailed for each project in the Getting Started box.

What is in this book
All projects are illustrated with several photographs to show you the detail of the work – both inspirational and useful for reference. A full summary of each project is given in the Getting Started box so you can see exactly what's involved. Here, projects are graded from one star (straightforward, suitable for beginners) through two (more challenging) to three stars (for crocheters with more confidence and experience).

Also in the Getting Started box is the size of each finished item, yarn(s) and additional materials needed, and what tension the project is worked in. Finally, a breakdown of the steps involved is given so you know exactly what the project entails before you start.

At the start of the pattern instructions is a key to all abbreviations particular to the project and occasional notes expand if necessary.

Additional information
Occasionally, more information is needed, or a slightly specialist technique is used. Pompoms, for example, feature several times, and detailed instructions for how to make them are given in the Making up paragraph on page 63.

If you have enjoyed the projects here, you may want to explore the other titles in the Easy Crochet series: *Babies & Children*, *Country*, *Flowers*, *Seaside* and *Vintage & Retro*. For those who enjoy knitting, a sister series, Easy Knitting, features similarly stylish yet simple projects.

Multi-colour cushions

Pick 'n' mix colours and styles to give your sofa the designer look.

Mix 'n' match styles with this set of zingy cushions. There is a small textured rib-patterned cushion with an envelope fastening, mid-sized lacy cushions featuring contrast linings and zip fastenings, and a large striped cushion, also with an envelope fastening.

The Yarn
Debbie Bliss Stella (approx. 88m/96 yards per 50g/1¾oz ball) is a luxurious mix of 60% silk, 20% rayon and 20% cotton in a chunky weight so it works up quickly. It can be machine washed at a low temperature and the colour palette has natural shades and bright colours.

GETTING STARTED

⭐ *Ribbed and striped cushions are straightforward treble fabrics and the lace pattern is easy.*

Size:
Ribbed cushion measures 30cm (12in) square
Lace cushion measures 40cm (16in) square
Striped cushion measures 50cm (20in) square

How much yarn:
Ribbed 4 x 50g (1¾oz) balls of Debbie Bliss Stella in Bright Pink (shade 08)
Lace 4 x 50g (1¾oz) balls of Debbie Bliss Stella in Lime (shade 15) or Orange (shade 06)
Striped 4 x 50g (1¾oz) balls of Debbie Bliss Stella in each of colour A – Turquoise (shade 12) and colour B – Pale Blue (shade 11)

Hook:
5.50mm (UK 5) crochet hook

Additional items:
Ribbed 3 large buttons, 30cm (12in) square cushion pad
Lace 42 x 82cm (16½ x 32in) cotton lining fabric, 40cm (16in) zip, sewing thread, 40cm (16in) square cushion pad
Striped 4 large buttons, 50cm (20in) square cushion pad

Tension:
Ribbed 13 sts and 9 rows measure 10cm (4in) square
Lace 15 sts and 7 rows measure 10cm (4in) square
Striped 13sts and 7 rows measure 10cm (4in) square for all cushions over patt using 5.50mm (UK 5) hook
IT IS ESSENTIAL TO WORK TO THE STATED TENSION TO ACHIEVE SUCCESS

What you have to do:
Ribbed Work throughout in trebles with relief trebles to form vertical 'ribs'. Work buttonhole border in double crochet. Construct envelope opening with button fastenings.
Lace Work simple lace pattern. Make up lining and sew in zip fastener.
Striped Work in trebles changing colour every 2 rows. Work buttonhole border in double crochet. Construct envelope opening.

Instructions

Abbreviations:
beg = beginning
ch = chain(s)
cm = centimetre(s)
dc = double crochet
patt = pattern
rep = repeat
RS = right side
st(s) = stitch(es)
tr = treble(s)
tr/rb = relief treble back
tr/rf = relief treble front
V-st = work 1 treble,
1 chain and 1 treble
into next stitch
WS = wrong side
yrh = yarn round hook

RIBBED CUSHION
(Worked in one piece)
With 5.50mm (UK 5) hook make 42ch.
Foundation row: (RS) 1tr into 4th ch from hook, 1tr into each ch to end, turn. 40tr.
1st row: 2ch (counts as first tr), miss 1tr, 1tr into each of next 3tr, *into each of next 2tr work: yrh, insert hook from right to left through stem of next st on back of work, pull loop through and complete tr as normal – called tr/rb, 1tr into each of next 4tr, rep from * to end, working last tr into top of turning ch, turn.
2nd row: 2ch, miss 1tr, 1tr into each of next 3tr, *into each of next 2tr work: yrh, insert hook from right to left through stem of next st on front of work, pull loop through and complete tr as normal – called tr/rf, 1tr into each of next 4tr, rep from * to end, working last tr into top of turning ch, turn.
The last 2 rows form patt. Rep them until work measures 70cm (27½in) from beg,

ending with a 2nd row.
Buttonhole border:
1st row: 1ch (counts as first dc), miss 1tr, 1dc into each tr to end, working last dc into top of turning ch, turn.
2nd row: 1ch, miss 1dc, 1dc into each of next 6dc, (2ch, miss 2dc, 1dc into each of next 10dc) twice, 2ch, miss 2dc, 1dc into each st to end, turn.
3rd row: 1ch, miss 1dc, 1dc into each dc to end, working 2dc into each 2ch space for buttonhole. Fasten off.

LACE CUSHIONS
Back:
With 5.50mm (UK 5) hook make 58ch.
Foundation row: (RS) V-st into 5th ch from hook, *miss 2ch, V-st into next ch, rep from * to last 2ch, miss 1ch, 1tr into last ch, turn.
1st row: 3ch (counts as first tr), *miss 2 sts, 3tr into 1ch sp on next V-st, rep from * to end, working last tr into top of turning ch, turn.

2nd row: 3ch, *miss 2tr, V-st into next tr (centre st of 3tr worked on previous row), rep from * to last st, miss this st, 1tr into turning ch, turn. The last 2 rows form patt. Rep them until work measures 40cm (16in) from beg. Fasten off.

Front:
Work as given for Back.

STRIPED CUSHION
(Worked in one piece)
With 5.5mm (UK 5) hook and A, make 67ch.
Foundation row: (RS) 1tr into 4ch ch from hook, 1tr into each tr to end, turn. 65 sts.
1st row: 3ch (counts as first tr), miss 1tr, 1tr into each tr to end, work last tr into top of turning ch, turn.
Rep last row to form patt, working in stripes of 2 rows each B and A until 38 stripes in all have been completed and ending with 2 rows in B.

Buttonhole border:
1st row: With A, 1ch (counts as first dc), miss 1tr, 1dc into each tr to end, working last dc into top of turning ch, turn.
2nd row: 1ch, miss 1dc, 1dc into each of next 11dc, (2ch, miss 2dc, 1dc into each of next 11dc) 3 times, 2ch, miss 2dc, 1dc into each st to end, turn.
3rd row: 1ch, miss 1dc, 1dc into each dc to end, working 2dc into each 2ch space for buttonhole. Fasten off.

Making up

RIBBED CUSHION
Place cover WS down with buttonhole border at top edge and fold over 11cm (4¼in) at top edge. Now bring lower edge up over top of flap so that edge is level with top fold. (The cover should measure 30 x 30cm (12 x 12in) so adjust two folds if necessary.) Join side seams, working through all thicknesses at flap. Turn RS out and sew on buttons to correspond with buttonholes.

LACE CUSHIONS
Turn and press 1cm (⅜in) to WS along short ends of lining fabric and insert zip into this edge. Open zip and turn lining WS out. With RS facing and zip at one edge, fold at the other, stitch lining free edges together taking 1cm (⅜in) seam. Press flat and turn lining RS out through zip opening.
Join top and side seams on front and back panels. Slide lining into crochet cover. Using sewing thread, slip stitch lower open edge in place to lining on either side of zip. Insert cushion pad and close zip.

STRIPED CUSHION
Place cover WS down with buttonhole border at top edge and fold over border plus 9 rows at top edge so that stripes match at side edges. Now bring lower edge up over top of flap so that edge is level with top fold and stripes match at side edges. (The cover should measure 50 x 50cm/20 x 20in.) Join side seams, working through all thicknesses at flap. Turn RS out and sew on buttons to correspond with buttonholes.

Pull-on hat

Two contrasting patterns are used for this striking and feminine beanie hat.

This beanie hat is worked in the round with a dense fabric of basic stitches for the crown and edged with a deep band of pretty lacy shells worked in two colours.

GETTING STARTED

⭐⭐ *Working in rounds will be unfamiliar at first, and pay attention to the shaping.*

Size:

To fit head: 51[56:61]cm (20[22:24]in) in circumference

Note: *Figures in square brackets [ ] refer to larger sizes; where there is only one set of figures, it applies to all sizes*

How much yarn:

1[1:2] x 50g (1¾oz) balls of Patons Diploma Gold DK in colour A – Cream (shade 6142)

1[1:1] ball in colour B – New Berry (shade 6239)

Hooks:

3.75mm (UK 9) crochet hook

4.00mm (UK 8) crochet hook

Tension:

First 4 rounds measure 7.5cm (3in) in diameter worked on 4.00mm (UK 8) hook

IT IS ESSENTIAL TO WORK TO THE STATED TENSION TO ACHIEVE SUCCESS

What you have to do:

Make five chains for centre of crown and slip stitch into first chain to form a circle. Work crown in one colour and alternating rounds of double crochet and trebles, increasing at regular intervals to shape hat. Join in a second colour and work shell edging in rounds, alternating the two colours each round.

The Yarn

Patons Diploma Gold DK (approx. 120m/136 yards per 50g/1¾oz ball) is a practical mix of 55% wool, 25% acrylic and 20% nylon. It is machine washable in plenty of shades.

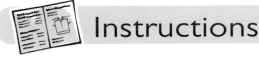 ## Instructions

With 4.00mm (UK 8) hook and A, make 5ch, join into a circle with a ss into first ch.

1st round: (Working into circle and over starting tail of yarn at same time), 1ch (counts as first dc), 11dc into ring, join with a ss into first ch. 12dc.

2nd round: 3ch (counts as first tr), 2tr into each of 11dc, 1tr into last dc, join with a ss into 3rd of 3ch. 24tr.

3rd round: 1ch, (1dc into next tr, 2dc into next tr) 11 times, 1dc into each of last 2tr, join with a ss into first ch. 36dc.

4th round: 3ch, (1tr into each of next 2dc, 2tr into next dc) 11 times, 1tr into each of last 3dc, join with a ss into 3rd of 3ch. 48tr.

5th round: 1ch, (1dc into each of next 5tr, 2dc into next tr) 7 times, 1dc into each of next 6tr, join with a ss into first ch. 56dc.

6th round: 3ch, (1tr into each of next 6dc, 2tr into next

Abbreviations:
beg = beginning
ch = chain(s)
cm = centimetre(s)
dc = double crochet
rep = repeat
sp = space
ss = slip stitch
st(s) = stitch(es)
tr = treble(s)

dc) 7 times, 1tr into each of next 7dc, join with a ss into 3rd of 3ch. 64tr.

7th round: 1ch, miss first tr, 1dc into each tr, join with a ss into first ch.

8th round: 3ch, (1tr into each of next 7dc, 2tr into next dc) 7 times, 1tr into each of next 8dc, join with a ss into 3rd of 3ch. 72tr.

9th round: As 7th round.

10th round: 3ch, (1tr into each of next 8dc, 2tr into next dc) 7 times, 1tr into each of next 9dc, join with a ss into 3rd of 3ch. 80tr.

11th round: As 7th round.

2nd and 3rd sizes only:

12th round: 3ch, (1tr into each of next 9dc, 2tr into next dc) 7 times, 1tr into each of next 10dc, join with a ss into 3rd of 3ch. 88tr.

13th round: As 7th round.

3rd size only:

14th round: 3ch, (1tr into each of next 10dc, 2tr into next dc) 7 times, 1tr into each of next 11dc, join with a ss into 3rd of 3ch. 96tr.

15th round: As 7th round.

All sizes:

80[88:96] sts.

Next round: 3ch, miss first dc, 1tr into each dc, join with a ss into 3rd of 3ch.

Next round: As 7th round.

Rep last 2 rounds until hat measures 12.5[14:15]cm (5[5½:6]in) from centre to outside edge, ending with a round of dc and changing to B for final ss of last round.

Note: Do not fasten off yarn after each round, but strand them up inside the hat.

1st round: With B, 4ch, 2tr into first dc, *miss 3dc, (2tr, 1ch, 2tr) into next dc, rep from * ending with 1tr into same place as base of 4ch, change to A, join with a ss into 3rd of 4ch.

2nd round: With A, ss into 1ch sp, 4ch, 2tr into same sp, *miss 4tr, (2tr, 1ch, 2tr) into 1ch sp, rep from * ending with 1tr into same sp as beg of round, change to B, join with a ss into 3rd of 4ch.

HOW TO
WORK IN THE ROUND

Instead of working in rows you can work crochet by starting with a central ring and continuing outwards in rounds. The right side of the work will be facing you all the time as you work.

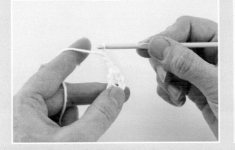

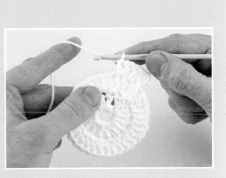

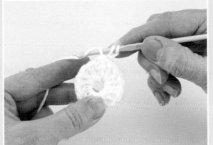

1 Begin by working the specified number of chains; join the first to the last with a slip stitch (or make a magic circle, see page 21). Hold the bottom of the loop between your thumb and forefinger and make the starting chain.

2 Work the first round directly into the loop ring.

3 To close the round, work a slip stitch into the top of the starting chain.

4 Make the required starting chain and then continue working the next round making each stitch as instructed by working under both loops of the stitch in the round below.

5 Continue in this way, working each round and joining the rounds with a slip stitch into the starting chain.

6 Working each round as instructed, the number of stitches in each round is increased so that the circle of stitches grows in size.

3rd round: With B, work as 2nd round, changing to A for final ss. Rep last 2 rounds twice more. Fasten off B.

Change to 3.75mm (UK 9) hook.
Next round: With A, ss into 1ch sp, 4ch, 1dc into same sp, *1ch, miss 2tr, 1dc into sp between 2 groups of tr, 1ch, miss 2tr, (1dc, 3ch, 1dc) into next 1ch sp, rep from * ending with 1ch, miss 2tr, 1dc into sp between 2 groups of tr, 1ch, join with a ss into first ch. Fasten off.

Making up

Darn in all yarn ends. Press lightly according to directions on ball band.

Giant scarf

Worked in thick yarn on a large hook, this long scarf is made in no time!

Made extra long for winding round your neck, this fabulous scarf has an eye-catching large openwork pattern and long fringes.

GETTING STARTED

Although chunky yarn works up quickly, the pattern needs concentration.

Size:
Scarf measures 24cm (9½in) wide x 204cm (80in) long, excluding fringing

How much yarn:
9 x 50g (1¾oz) balls of Debbie Bliss Como in Rose Pink (shade 10)

Hook:
9.00mm (UK 00) crochet hook

Tension:
9 sts (1 patt rep) measure 11cm (4¼in) and 4 rows (1 patt rep) measure 7.5cm (3in) on 9.00mm (UK 00) hook
IT IS ESSENTIAL TO WORK TO THE STATED TENSION TO ACHIEVE SUCCESS

What you have to do:
Make long length of chain for foundation chain. Work foundation row and last row (long side edges) in double crochet. Work three repeats of motif pattern with large clusters and chain spaces. Work two rows of double crochet along short ends. Add tassels to short ends of scarf.

The Yarn
Debbie Bliss Como (approx. 42m/46 yards per 50g/1¾oz ball) is a luxurious blend of 90% wool and 10% cashmere in a chunky weight. It is softly spun and looks good in large, distinctive patterns such as this. The colours are mainly subtle shades.

Instructions

Abbreviations:
ch = chain(s)
cl = cluster(s)
cm = centimetre(s)
cont = continue
dc = double crochet
patt = pattern
rep = repeat
RS = right side
sp = space(s)
ss = slip stitch
st(s) = stitch(es)
tr = treble(s)
yrh = yarn round hook

SCARF:
With 9.00mm (UK 00) hook make 168ch.

Foundation row: (RS) 1dc into 2nd ch from hook, 1dc into each ch to end, turn. 167dc.

1st row: 3ch (counts as first tr), work 2tr into first st leaving last loop of each on hook, yrh and draw through all 3 loops on hook – called 2tr cl, *miss 3 sts, 2tr cl in next st, 3ch, ss into same st as last cl, 5ch, miss 4 sts, ss into next st, 3ch, 2tr cl into same st as ss, rep from * to last 4 sts, miss 3 sts, 2tr cl into last st, 3ch, ss into same st as cl, turn.

2nd row: 3ch, *work 3tr in top of next cl leaving last loop of each on hook, yrh and draw through all 4 loops on hook – called 3tr cl, 3ch, 3tr cl in same place as last 3tr cl, 2ch, ss into 3rd of 5ch, 2ch, rep from * ending last rep with (3tr cl, 3ch, 3tr cl) into top of next cl, turn.

3rd row: 1ch, *5dc into 3ch sp between cl of previous row, 4ch, rep from * ending last rep with 5dc into last 3ch sp, turn.

4th row: 1ch, *1dc into each of next 5 sts, 4dc into 4ch sp, rep from * ending 1dc into each of last 5 sts, turn.

Rep last 4 rows twice more. Fasten off.
With RS of work facing, rejoin yarn to one short end of Scarf and work 17dc along row ends. Work 1 more row in dc. Fasten off. Complete other short end of Scarf in same way.

Tassels:
Cut 5 x 35cm (14in) lengths of yarn for each tassel. Knot 5 tassels evenly across each short end of Scarf. Trim tassels.

Cake selection

Serve up a teatime treat with these funky crochet cakes.

Traditional British teatime favourites – without the calories – make an amusing decoration for the table.

GETTING STARTED

⭐⭐ *Easy stitches but care is needed with construction.*

Size:

Slice of Victoria sponge: 12cm (4¾in) tall x 11cm (4¼in) long x 7cm (2¾in) at widest point

Vanilla slice: 4.5cm (1¾in) x 10cm (4in) x 4.5cm (1¾in) deep

Slice of Battenberg: 9cm (3½in) square x 2.5cm (1in) deep

Apricot Danish pastry: 10cm (4in) square x 3.5cm (1⅜in) deep

Cherry Bakewell: 8cm (3⅛in) in diameter x 5cm (2in) deep (3⅛ x 2in)

Note: *All measurements are approximate*

How much yarn:

For all five cakes:

1 x 100g (3½oz) ball of Patons Fab DK in each of three colours: A – Beige (shade 02331); B – Cream (shade 02307) and C – White (shade 02306)

1 x 25g (1oz) ball of Patons FaB DK in each of six colours: D – Red (shade 02322); E – Camel (shade 02308); F – Brown (shade 02309); G – Pink (shade 02304); H – Lemon (shade 02330) and I – Canary (shade 02305)

Hook:

4.00mm (UK 8) crochet hook

Additional items:

Stitch markers

Foam block for cutting to shape

Polyester toy filling

Tension:

20 sts and 22 rows measure 10cm (4in) square over dc on 4.00mm (UK 8) hook

What you have to do:

Work individual cakes in colours specified and mainly simple stitches, including double crochet, half trebles and trebles. Work in rows or rounds as specified. Follow instructions for simple increasing or decreasing to shape cakes. Construct cakes following instructions, adding block of foam or polyester filling.

The Yarn

Patons FaB DK is 100% acrylic. Popular shades come in 100g (3½oz) balls (approx. 274m/299 yards per ball); plenty of colours come in 25g (1oz) balls (approx. 68m/74 yards per ball).

 Instructions

VICTORIA SPONGE SLICE:

Outer gateau piece:

With 4.00mm (UK 8) hook and A, make 4ch.

1st row: 3tr in 4th ch from hook, turn. 4 sts.

2nd row: 3ch (counts as first tr), 1tr in st at base of ch, 1tr in each st to end, working last tr in 3rd of 3ch, turn. 1 st inc at beg of row.

3rd–10th rows: As 2nd row. 13 sts.

11th row: 3ch, miss st at base of ch, 1tr in front loop only of each st to end, turn.

12th row: 3ch, miss st at base of ch, 1tr in each st to end, joining in D on last st, turn.

13th row: With D, 2ch, miss st at base of ch, 1htr in each st to end, joining in C on last st, turn. Cut off D.

14th row: With C, 2ch, miss st at base of ch, 1htr in front loop only of each st to end, changing to A on last st, turn. Cut off C.

15th row: With A, as 11th row.

16th row: Work in tr.

17th row: 3ch, miss st at base of ch, 1tr in front loop only of each of next 10 sts, tr2tog over last st and top of turning ch, turn. 1 st dec at end of row.

18th row: 3ch, miss st at base of ch, 1tr into each st to last 2 sts, tr2tog over last st and top of turning ch, turn. 1 st dec at end of row.

19th–25th rows: As 18th row. 4 sts.

26th row: 3ch, miss st at base of ch, tr3tog. Fasten off.

Cake sides piece:

With 4.00mm (UK 8) hook and B, make 45ch.

1st row: 1tr in 4th ch from hook, 1tr in each ch to end, turn. 43 sts.

2nd row: 2ch (counts as first htr), miss st at base of ch, 1htr in each st to end, working last htr in top of turning ch and joining in D on last st, turn.

3rd row: With D, work in htr, joining in C on last st. Cut off D.

Abbreviations:

beg = beginning;

ch = chain(s);

cm = centimetre(s)

dc = double crochet;

dc2tog = (insert hook in next st, yrh and draw a loop through) twice, yrh and draw through all 3 loops on hook;

dec = decrease;

foll = follows;

htr = half treble

inc = increased;

rem = remaining;

rep = repeat

RS = right side;

rtrb = relief treble back as foll: yrh, insert hook from right to left and from back around post of next st, yrh and complete tr in usual way;

ss = slip stitch;

st(s) = stitch(es)

tr = treble;

tr2(3)tog = work 1tr in each of next 2(3) sts leaving last loop of each of hook, yrh and draw through all 3(4) loops

WS = wrong side;

yrh = yarn round hook

Note: To make a Magic Circle, wrap yarn clockwise around forefinger twice to form a ring. Holding end of yarn between thumb and middle finger, insert hook into ring and draw yarn from ball through.

4th row: With C, work 1htr in front loop only of each st, changing to B on last st. Cut off C.

5th row: With B, work 1htr in front loop only of each st to end, turn.

6th row: 3ch, miss st at base of ch, work in tr to end. Fasten off.

Cream swirl:

With 4.00mm (UK 8) hook and C, make a magic circle (see Note right).

1st round: (10ch, 1dc in circle) 9 times, 6ch. Fasten off, leaving a long end. Pull on yarn end to tighten circle and close hole. Thread tail in yarn needle, then take yarn through 5th ch of each loop and back through top of 6ch. Draw yarn up until loops gather towards centre but leaving an internal circle of about 2cm (¾in). Turn swirl upside down to assess size and tighten or loosen yarn accordingly. Make knot to fasten off but leave yarn tail for attaching decoration to cake.

Strawberry:

With 4.00mm (UK 8) hook and D, make a magic circle.

1st round: 1ch, work 6dc in circle, join with a ss in first dc. If using st marker, start marking beg of each round.

2nd round: (2dc in next st, 1dc in each of next 2 sts) to end. 8 sts.

3rd round: (2dc in next st, 1dc in each of next 3 sts) to end. 10 sts.

4th round: (2dc in next st, 1dc in each of next 4 sts) to end. 12 sts.

5th round: As 3rd. 15 sts.

6th round: As 2nd. 20 sts.

7th round: As 4th. 24 sts.

8th round: (Dc2tog over next 2 sts, 1dc in next st) to end. 16 sts.

9th round: (Dc2tog over next 2 sts) to end. 8 sts. Fasten off. Turn inside out, stuff, then gather up yarn around edge of opening, draw up tight and fasten off. Use C to embroider small 'pips' on strawberry.

VANILLA SLICE:
Top and bottom rectangles:
(make 2)

With 4.00mm (UK 8) hook and B, make 10ch.

1st row: 1tr in 4th ch from hook, 1tr in each ch to end, turn. 8 sts.

2nd–9th rows: 3ch (counts as first tr), miss st at base of ch, 1tr in each st to end, working last tr in 3rd of 3ch, turn. Fasten off.

Long side strip:

With 4.00mm (UK 8) hook and B, make 53ch.

1st row: 1htr in 3rd ch from hook, 1htr in each ch to end, turn. 52 sts.

2nd row: 2ch (counts as first htr), miss st at base of ch, 1htr in each st to end, working last htr in 2nd of 2ch. Fasten off.

Pastry layers: (make 2 with E and 1 with A)

Work as given for Top and bottom rectangles.

Icing layer:

With 4.00mm (UK 8) hook and C, make 10ch.

1st row: (RS) 1tr in 4th ch from hook, 1tr in each ch to end, joining in F on last st, turn. 8 sts. Cut off C.

2nd row: With F, 1ch (counts as first dc), miss st at base of ch, 1dc in each of next 3 sts, 1rtrb around next st, 1dc in each of next 3 sts, joining in C on last st, turn. Cut off F.

3rd row: With C, 3ch, miss st at base of ch, 1tr in each st to end, joining in F on last st, turn. Cut off C.

4th–11th rows: Rep 2nd and 3rd rows 4 times more. Fasten off.

BATTENBERG SLICE:

Cake top: (make 2 with G and 2 with H)

With 4.00mm (UK 8) hook make 9ch.

1st row: 1dc in 2nd ch from hook, 1dc in each ch to end, turn. 8 sts.

2nd–8th rows: 1ch (counts as first dc), miss st at base of ch, 1dc in each st to end, turn. Fasten off.

Cake base:

With 4.00mm (UK 8) hook and B, make 17ch. Work 16 rows in dc on 16 sts as given for Cake top. Fasten off.

Cake side:

With 4.00mm (UK 8) hook and B, make 5ch. Work 64 rows in dc on 4 sts as given for Cake top. Fasten off.

APRICOT DANISH PASTRY:

Pastry inner layer:

With 4.00mm (UK 8) hook and B, make 23ch.

1st row: 1tr in 4th ch from hook, 1tr in each ch to end, turn. 21 sts.

2nd row: 3ch (counts as first tr), miss st at base of ch, 1tr in each st to end, working last tr in 3rd of 3ch, turn.

3rd–11th rows: As 2nd row. Fasten off.

Pastry outer layer:

With 4.00mm (UK 8) hook and A, make 23ch. Work 11 rows in tr as given for inner layer, joining in E at end of last row. Cut off A.

Edging:

With E, 2ch, work in htr around outer edges of square, working 2htr in each corner st, join with a ss in 2nd of 2ch. Fasten off.

Apricot half:

With 4.00mm (UK 8) hook and I, make a magic circle.

1st round: 1ch, work 6dc in circle, join with a ss in first dc. If using st marker, start marking beg of each round.

2nd round: 2dc in each st to end. 12 sts.

3rd round: (2dc in next st, 1dc in next st) to end. 18 sts.

4th round: Work in dc.

5th round: (2dc in next st, 1dc in each of next 2 sts) to end. 24 sts.

6th round: Work in dc.

7th round: (Dc2tog over next 2 sts) to end. 12 sts.

Lightly stuff apricot half to make a flattish dome.

8th round: As 7th round. 6 sts. Fasten off.
Icing drizzle:
With 4.00mm (UK 8) hook and C, make 80ch. Fasten off.

CHERRY BAKEWELL:
Cake top:
With 4.00mm (UK 8) hook and C, make a magic circle.
1st round: 1ch, work 7dc in circle, join with a ss in first dc. If using st marker, start marking beg of each round.
2nd round: 2dc in each st to end. 14 sts.
3rd round: (2dc in next st, 1dc in next st) to end. 21 sts.
4th round: (2dc in next st, 1dc in each of next 2 sts) to end. 28 sts.
5th round: (2dc in next st, 1dc in each of next 3 sts) to end. 35 sts.
6th round: (2dc in next st, 1dc in each of next 4 sts) to end. 42 sts.
7th round: (2dc in next st, 1dc in each of next 5 sts) to end. 49 sts.
8th round: Work in dc. Fasten off.
Cherry:
With 4.00mm (UK 8) hook and D, make a magic circle.
1st round: 1ch, work 6dc in circle, join with a ss in first dc. If using st marker, start marking beg of each round.
2nd round: (2dc in next st, 1dc in next st) to end. 9 sts.
3rd round: (2dc in next st, 1dc in each of next 2 sts) to end. 12 sts. Fasten off, leaving a long end. Sew cherry to centre of cake top.
Base:
(Worked with WS facing)
With A, work as given for cake top until 7th round has been completed. 49 sts.
8th round: 1ch, ss into each st to end.
9th round: (Working into front loop only of each st in this round, dc2tog, 1dc in each of next 5 sts) to end. 42 sts.
10th–12th rounds: Work in dc.
13th round: (2dc in next st, 1dc in each of next 5 sts) to end. 49 sts.
Join to cake top:
Next round: Place cake top in centre of base, inserting hook through st on edge of cake top and next st along base work 1dc, matching up cake top and base, cont to work 1dc through pairs of sts until 30 sts have been worked; stuff cake with polyester filling before completing rem pairs of sts to close gap.
Edging:
Next round: Ss in next st, (2dc in next st, ss in next st) to end. Fasten off.

Making up

VICTORIA SPONGE SLICE:
Fold cake sides piece in half and mark centre. Align short ends with back of outer gateau piece, using red and white stripes as a guide. Pin, then sew matched-up edges in place. Match points at start and end of outer gateau piece to marker at centre of cake sides piece and pin edges in place. Sew three of the four edges. Either cut a foam wedge to shape or stuff firmly with polyester filling. Join rem edge.
With D, sew strawberry to cream swirl, then use yarn tail of C to sew decoration to top of cake.

VANILLA SLICE:
Join ends of long side strip then sew one edge around bottom rectangle. Cut foam block to fit, or stuff firmly with polyester filling, then sew top rectangle to other side of long strip. Sew a pastry layer in E, then another in A on bottom rectangle. Sew a pastry layer in E, then icing layer on top rectangle.

BATTENBURG SLICE:
Using picture as a guide and G, sew four small squares of cake top together. Join short ends of cake side together, then fold in half (with join at one side) and then in half again and mark quarter points with pins. Matching quarter points to corners of base square, sew cake side in place. Then sew cake top in place around three sides, leaving one side open. Stuff cake firmly with polyester filling or cut foam block to fit, before neatly slipstitching last side closed.

APRICOT DANISH PASTRY:
Place pastry inner layer on top of outer layer. Place apricot half in centre of squares as a guide, then fold in four corners of squares to middle just under outer edge of apricot and sew corners in place. Attach apricot half to centre of folded squares, ensuring that stitches do not show through on to bottom of pastry. Place icing drizzle as required and sew in place. 'Puff' up pastry by cupping cake in hands to bring up edges slightly.

Fingerless mitts

Crochet this fashionable accessory: mitts that
can be worn with your favourite jacket or coat.

These long, fingerless mitts in a straightforward slightly openwork pattern have cuffs worked in relief trebles with a ribbed appearance.

GETTING STARTED

Pattern is not too difficult as there are no fingers to shape, but it does require concentration for thumb shaping.

Size:
To fit an adult woman's hand

How much yarn:
2 x 50g (1¾oz) balls of Debbie Bliss Rialto DK in Purple (shade 16)

Hook:
4.00mm (UK 8) crochet hook

Tension:
16 sts and 12 rows measure 10cm (4in) square over main patt on 4.00mm (UK 8) hook
IT IS ESSENTIAL TO WORK TO THE STATED TENSION TO ACHIEVE SUCCESS

What you have to do:
Make foundation chain and join into a circle. Work foundation round of treble. Work 'cuff' in mock ribbing comprising relief trebles. Work main pattern of V stitches, shaping for thumb as instructed. Leave stitches for thumb and continue main part, finishing with double crochet edging. Return to thumb stitches and complete thumb.

The Yarn
Debbie Bliss Rialto DK (approx. 105m/114 yards per 50g/1¾oz ball) contains 100% merino wool. This yarn is soft and warm and can be machine washed at a low temperature, so is perfect for these mitts. There are plenty of great shades to choose from.

Instructions

Abbreviations:

beg = beginning
ch = chain(s)
cm = centimetre(s)
cont = continue
dc = double crochet
foll = follows
patt = pattern
rep = repeat
RS = right side
tr/rb(f) = relief treble back(front)
sp = space
ss = slip stitch
st(s) = stitch(es)
tr = treble(s)
WS = wrong side
yrh = yarn round hook

RIGHT MITT:

With 4.00mm (UK 8) hook make 40ch, ss into first ch to form a circle.

Foundation round: (WS) 3ch, miss first ch, 1tr into each ch to end, join with a ss into 3rd of 3ch at beg of round, turn. 40 sts.

1st round: 2ch (counts as first tr), *yrh, insert hook from in front and right to left round stem of next st and complete tr in normal way – called 1tr/rf, yrh, insert hook from behind and from right to left round stem of next st and complete tr in normal way – called 1tr/rb, rep from * to last st, 1tr/rf round stem of last st, join with a ss into 2nd of 2ch, turn.

2nd round: 2ch (counts as first tr), *1tr/rb round stem of next st, 1tr/rf round stem of next st, rep from * to last st, 1tr/rb round stem of last st, join with a ss into 2nd of 2ch, turn.

Rep 1st and 2nd rounds twice more, then work 1st round again, do not turn at end of last round.

Dec round: 1ch (counts as first dc), miss next st, 1dc into next st, (1dc into next st, miss next st, 1dc into next st) 6 times, miss next st, (1dc into next st, miss next st, 1dc into next st) 6 times, join with a ss into first ch, do not turn. 26 sts.

Cont in main patt as foll:

1st round: (RS) 3ch, 1tr into st at base of 3ch, *miss next st, 2tr into next st – called V st, rep from * to end, join with a ss into 3rd of 3ch, turn.

2nd round: Ss into centre of V st, 3ch, 1tr into same V st, *2tr into centre of next V st, rep from * to end, join with a ss into 3rd of 3ch, turn.

Rep last round 6 times more. **

Shape for thumb:

Next round: (RS) Patt 16 sts, work 2tr into sp between last V st and next V st (inc made), patt rem 10 sts, join with a ss into 3rd of 3ch, turn. 28 sts.

Next round: Patt 10 sts, work 2tr into sp between last V st and next V st, work 2tr into centre of next V st, work 2tr into sp between last V st and next V st, patt rem 16 sts, join with a ss into 3rd of 3ch, turn. 32 sts.

Next round: Patt 18 sts, work 2tr into sp between last V st and next V st, work 2tr into centre of next V st, work 2tr into sp between last V st and next V st, patt rem 12 sts, join with a ss into 3rd of 3ch, turn. 36 sts.

Patt 6 rounds without shaping.

Next round: (WS) Patt 10 sts, leave next 10 sts for thumb, patt rem 16 sts, join with a ss into 3rd of 3ch, turn. 26 sts. Cont on these 26 sts only, patt 3 rounds.

Next round: 1ch, 1dc into each st to end, join with a ss into first ch, turn. Work 1 round in dc. Fasten off.

Thumb:

Rejoin yarn to 10 sts left for thumb. Work 1 round in main patt, then 2 rounds in dc. Fasten off.

LEFT MITT:

Work as given for Right mitt to **.

Shape for thumb:

Next round: (RS) Patt 10 sts, work 2tr into sp between last V st and next V st (inc made), patt rem 16 sts, join with a ss into 3rd of 3ch, turn. 28 sts.

Next round: Patt 16 sts, work 2tr into sp between last V st and next V st, work 2tr into centre of next V st, work 2tr into sp between last V st and next V st, patt rem 10 sts, join with a ss into 3rd of 3ch, turn. 32 sts.

Next round: Patt 12 sts, work 2tr into sp between last V st and next V st, work 2tr into centre of next V st, work 2tr into sp between last V st and next V st, patt rem 18 sts, join with a ss into 3rd of 3ch, turn. 36 sts.

Patt 6 rounds without shaping.

Next round: (WS) Patt 16 sts, leave next 10 sts for thumb, patt rem 10 sts, join with a ss into 3rd of 3ch, turn. 26 sts. Cont on these 26 sts only, patt 3 rounds.

Next round: 1ch, 1dc into each st to end, join with a ss into first ch, turn. Work 1 round in dc. Fasten off.

Thumb:

Rejoin yarn to 10 sts left for thumb.
Work 1 round in main patt, then 2 rounds in dc. Fasten off.

Square beanie

Equally at home on the streets, at the beach or in the country, this hat will become a firm favourite.

With its square crown of textured stitches and smooth sides worked in rounds of trebles, this handy hat will prove popular with the man in your life as well.

The Yarn
Debbie Bliss Rialto DK (approx. 105m/114 yards per 50g/1¾oz ball) contains 100% merino wool. This luxurious yarn produces an attractive fabric, machine-washable at a low temperature, and you can choose from a wide colour palette.

GETTING STARTED

★★ Working relief stitches requires concentration.

Size:
To fit an average-sized woman's head; circumference approximately 53cm (21in)

How much yarn:
2 x 50g (1¾oz) balls of Debbie Bliss Rialto DK in Teal Blue (shade 39)

Hooks:
3.50mm (UK 9) crochet hook
4.00mm (UK 8) crochet hook

Tension:
18 sts and 10 rows measure 10cm (4in) square over rounds of tr on 4.00mm (UK 8) hook
IT IS ESSENTIAL TO WORK TO THE STATED TENSION TO ACHIEVE SUCCESS

What you have to do:
Working in rounds of relief double trebles, start at centre of crown and work a square. Continue in rounds of trebles, without further increasing, for sides of hat. Finish with a border of relief trebles to form a mock rib.

Instructions

Abbreviations:

ch = chain

cm = centimetre(s)

dtr = double treble

foll = following

rdtrf = relief dtr front: inserting hook from right to left and from front to back, work 1dtr around stem of st indicated

rep = repeat

rtrb = relief tr back: inserting hook from right to left and from back to front, work 1tr around stem of st indicated

rtrb2tog =work 1 rtrb around stem of sts indicated, leaving last loop of each on hook, yrh and draw through all 3 loops

rtrf = relief tr front: inserting hook from right to left and from front to back, work 1tr around stem of st indicated

sp = space

ss = slip stitch

st(s) = stitch(es)

tr = treble

HAT:

With 4.00mm (UK 8) hook make 6ch, join with a ss into first ch to form a ring.

1st round: (Work over starting tail of yarn), 5ch (counts as 1tr, 2ch), (3tr into ring, 2ch) 3 times, 2tr into ring, join with a ss into 3rd of 5ch. Gently pull on starting tail to tighten centre of square.

2nd round: Ss into 2ch sp, 5ch, 2tr into same sp, *1rdtrf into next tr, 1tr into next tr, 1rdtrf into next tr, (2tr, 2ch, 2tr) into next 2ch sp, rep from * twice more, 1rdtrf into next tr, 1tr into next tr, 1rdtrf into next tr, 1tr into first ch sp, join with a ss into 3rd of 5ch. 7 sts on each side.

3rd round: Ss into 2ch sp, 5ch, 2tr into same sp, *(1rdtrf into next tr, 1tr into next tr) 3 times, 1rdtrf into next tr, (2tr, 2ch, 2tr) into next 2ch sp, rep from * twice more, (1rdtrf into next tr, 1tr into next tr) 3 times, 1rdtrf into next tr, 1tr into first ch sp, join with a ss into 3rd of 5ch. 11 sts on each side.

4th round: Ss into 2ch sp, 5ch, 2tr into same sp, *(1rdtrf into next tr, 1tr into next tr) 5 times, 1rdtrf into next tr, (2tr, 2ch, 2tr) into next 2ch sp, rep from * twice more, (1rdtrf into next tr, 1tr into next tr) 5 times, 1rdtrf into next tr, 1tr into first ch sp, join with a ss into 3rd of 5ch. 15 sts on each side.

5th round: Ss into 2ch sp, 5ch, 2tr into same sp, *(1rdtrf into next tr, 1tr into next tr) 7 times, 1rdtrf into next tr, (2tr, 2ch, 2tr) into next 2ch sp, rep from * twice more, (1rdtrf into next tr, 1tr into next tr) 7 times, 1rdtrf into next tr, 1tr into first ch sp, join with a ss into 3rd of 5ch. 19 sts on each side.

7th round: Ss into 2ch sp, 3ch (counts as first tr), (1tr into each of next 23 sts, 1tr into 2ch sp) 3 times, 1tr into each of next 23 sts, join with a ss into 3rd of 3ch. 96 sts.

8th round: 3ch, miss st at base of ch, 1tr into each tr, join with a ss into 3rd of 3ch. Rep last round 11 more times.

Border:

Change to 3.50mm (UK 9) hook.

Next round: 2ch, miss st at base of ch, *1rtrf in next tr, rtrb2tog over next 2tr, (1rtrf in next tr, 1rtrb in foll tr) 6 times, 1rtrf in next tr, rtrb2tog over next 2tr, (1rtrf in next tr, 1rtrb in foll tr) 7 times, rep from * twice more, ending last rep (1rtrf, 1rtrb) 6 times, 1rtrf in last tr, join with a ss into 2nd of 2ch. 90 sts.

Next round: 2ch, *1rtrf in next rtrf, 1rtrb in next rtrb, rep from * all round (treating rtrb2tog as 1rtrb), ending 1rtrf in rtrf, join with a ss into 2nd of 2ch.

Rep last round 3 more times. Fasten off.

6th round: Ss into 2ch sp, 5ch, 2tr into same sp, *(1rdtrf into next tr, 1tr into next tr) 9 times, 1rdtrf into next tr, (2tr, 2ch, 2tr) into next 2ch sp, rep from * twice more, (1rdtrf into next tr, 1tr into next tr) 9 times, 1rdtrf into next tr, 1tr into first ch sp, join with a ss into 3rd of 5ch. 23 sts on each side.

Striped place mats

Simple to make, these stylish mats will colour co-ordinate your dining table.

These matching mats and coasters make stylish dining accessories. Worked in an easy stitch pattern, the textured stripes are enhanced by the dramatic colour contrast of black, white and fuchsia .

GETTING STARTED

⭐ *Simple stitch and stripe pattern with no shaping involved.*

Size:
Placemat: 35 x 25cm (13¾ x 10in)
Coaster: 14 x 14cm (5½ x 5½in)

How much yarn:
For four table settings:
2 x 100g (3½oz) balls of King Cole Bamboo Cotton in each of two colours: A – Black (shade 534) and B – White (shade 530)
1 ball of colour C – Fuchsia (shade 536)

Hook:
4.00mm (UK 8) crochet hook

Tension:
18 sts and 13 rows measure 10cm (4in) square over patt on 4.00mm (UK 8) hook
IT IS ESSENTIAL TO WORK TO THE STATED TENSION TO ACHIEVE SUCCESS

What you have to do:
Work foundation chain. Work pattern as instructed, changing colour every two rows. Carry colour not in use up side of work. Neaten edges with border of double crochet.

The Yarn
King Cole Bamboo Cotton (approx. 230m/251 yards per 100g/3½oz ball) is 50% bamboo and 50% cotton in a double knitting weight yarn, which can be machine washed.

Instructions

Abbreviations:

ch = chain(s)

cm = centimetre(s)

cont = continue

dc = double crochet

foll = follows

htr = half treble

patt = pattern

rep = repeat

RS = right side

ss = slip stitch

st(s) = stitch(es)

tr = treble

PLACEMAT:

With 4.00mm (UK 8) hook and A, make 46ch. Cont in alternate stripes of 2 rows A and 2 rows B, carrying yarn not in use up side of work.

Foundation row: (RS) With A, work 1dc into 2nd ch from hook, *1htr into next ch, 1tr into next ch, 1htr into next ch, 1dc into next ch, rep from * to end, turn.

1st row: With A, 1ch, 1dc into first dc, *1htr into next htr, 1tr into next tr, 1htr into next htr, 1dc into next dc, rep from * to end, turn (omitting turning ch).

2nd row: With B, 3ch (counts as first tr), miss first dc, *1htr into next htr, 1dc into next tr, 1htr into next htr, 1tr into next dc, rep from * to end, turn (omitting turning ch).

3rd row: With B, 3ch, miss first tr, *1htr into next htr, 1dc into next dc, 1htr into next htr, 1tr into next tr, rep from * to end, working last tr into 3rd of 3ch, turn.

4th row: With A, 1ch, 1dc into first tr, *1htr into next htr, 1tr into next dc, 1htr into next htr, 1dc into next tr, rep from * to end, working last dc into 3rd of 3ch, turn.

Rep 1st–4th rows 8 times more, then work 1st row again.

Cont in patt as set, work 8 more rows in

stripes as foll: 2 rows C, 2 rows B, 2 rows C and 2 rows A. Do not fasten off, but turn and cont as foll:

Edging:

With A, 1ch, work 1dc into each st to last (corner) st on this side, 2dc into corner st, cont in dc around rem 3 sides (working approximately 5dc into every 4 row ends) and 2dc into each corner st, ending 1dc into same place as first dc. Join with a ss into first ch. Fasten off.

COASTER:

With 4.00mm (UK 8) hook and A, make 26ch. Work foundation row and cont in patt as given for Placemat, working 18 rows in stripes as foll: 2 rows A, 2 rows B, 2 rows A, 2 rows C, 2 rows B, 2 rows C, 2 rows A, 2 rows B and 2 rows A. Fasten off.

Edging:

Work as given for Placemat.

Slouch socks

Perfect for keeping your toes cosy, these chunky socks
have bright striped tops.

With contrast-coloured heel and toe and striped, slouchy tops, these fun socks worked in double crochet and an elongated stitch pattern are bound to cheer you up.

GETTING STARTED

★ ★ *Stitches are straightforward but there is a lot of shaping to concentrate on.*

Size:
To fit shoe size: 4–5[5–6:6–7]
Foot length: 22[24:26]cm (8½[9½:10¼]in)
Note: Figures in square brackets [ ] refer to larger sizes; where there is only one set of figures, it applies to all sizes

How much yarn:
2[2:3] x 50g (1¾oz) balls of Debbie Bliss Baby Cashmerino in main colour A – Cream (shade 101)
1 ball in each three contrast colours: B – Pink (shade 029); C – Lilac (shade 033) and D – Turquoise (shade 031)

Hooks:
3.50mm (UK 9) crochet hook
4.00mm (UK 8) crochet hook

Tension:
21 elongated dc and 18 rows measure 10cm (4in) square on 3.50mm (UK 9) hook
IT IS ESSENTIAL TO WORK TO THE STATED TENSION TO ACHIEVE SUCCESS

What you have to do:
Work toe and heel in double crochet and foot in elongated dc in colours as instructed and shaping as directed. Work leg section in stripes and cluster pattern as directed. Work mainly in rounds (so no harsh seams or making up required).

The Yarn
Debbie Bliss Baby Cashmerino (approx. 125m/136 yards per 50g/1¾oz ball) contains 50% merino wool, 33% microfibre and 12% cashmere. It produces a soft, luxurious fabric that can be machine washed at a low temperature. There is an extensive shade palette.

Instructions

Abbreviations:

alt = alternate

beg = beginning

ch = chain(s)

cm = centimetre(s)

cont = continue

dc = double crochet

elongated dc = insert hook into next st and draw a loop through, yrh and draw through first loop on hook, yrh and draw through both loops on hook

foll = follow(s)(ing)

htr = half treble

inc = increase(ing)

patt = pattern

rep = repeat

sp(s) = space(s)

ss = slip stitch

st(s) = stitch(es)

tr = treble

yrh = yarn round hook

SOCKS: (make 2)

With 4.00mm (UK 8) hook and B, make 9[9:11]ch for toe.

1st round: Working into top loop only, work 1dc into 2nd ch from hook, 1dc into each of next 7[7:9]ch, now work 1dc into each loop along other side of ch. 18[18:22]dc.

2nd round: 1dc into first dc and mark this dc, work 2dc into next dc, (1dc inc), 1dc into each of next 6[6:8]dc, inc in next dc, 1dc into next dc and mark this dc, inc in next dc, 1dc into each of next 6[6:8] dc, inc in next dc (dc before marked dc). 22[22:26]dc.

Moving markers up on each round, work as foll:

3rd round: 1dc into each dc all round.

4th round: 1dc into first marked dc, inc in next dc, 1dc into each dc to within 1dc of next marked dc, inc in next dc, 1dc into marked dc, inc in next dc, 1dc into each dc to within 1dc of first marked dc, inc in next dc. 26[26:30]dc.

Cont to inc 4 dc in this way (1dc each side of marked dc) on every alt round until there are 34[38:46]dc, ending with a 3rd round. Remove second marker. Remaining marker indicates beg of rounds.

Cut off B and join in A. Change to 3.50mm (UK 9) hook. Work foot as foll:

Patt round: 1 elongated dc into each dc all round. Rep last round until Sock measures 14[16:18]cm (5½[6¼:7]in). (Length can be adjusted here and should be 8cm (3in) less than desired foot length, measured from back of heel to tip of toe.)

Place a marker on 18th[20th:24th]dc. Markers indicate sides of foot. Cont in elongated dc, working gusset by inc 1 st at each side of marked sts on next and every foll alt round until there are 54[58:66]dc. Remove markers.

Next row: Patt 12[13:15], do not turn but cut off A and join in C.

Now work heel in dc as foll:

Change to 4.00mm (UK 8) hook.

1st row: With C, work 2dc into next st, 1dc into next st, 2dc into next st, ss into next st, turn. 5dc.

2nd row: 1ch, 1dc into first dc, (inc in next dc, 1dc into next dc) twice, ss into next st of foot, turn. 7dc.

3rd row: 1ch, 1dc into each of next 2dc, inc in next dc, 1dc into next dc, inc in next dc, 1dc into each of next 2dc, ss into next st of foot, turn. 9dc.

4th row: 1ch, 1dc into each of next 3dc, inc in next dc, 1dc into next dc, inc in next dc, 1dc into each of next 3dc, ss into next st of foot, turn. 11dc.

5th row: 1ch, 1dc into each of next 4dc, inc in next dc, 1dc into next dc, inc in next dc, 1dc into each of next 4dc, ss into next st of foot, turn. 13dc.

6th row: 1ch, 1dc into each of next 5dc, inc in next dc, 1dc into next dc, inc in next dc, 1dc into each of next 5dc, ss into next st of foot, turn. 15dc.

3rd size only:

7th row: 1ch, 1dc into each of next 6dc, inc in next dc, 1dc into next dc, inc in next dc, 1dc into each of next 6dc, ss into next st of foot, turn. 17dc.

All sizes:

Next row: 1ch, 1dc into each of next 15[15:17]dc, ss into next st of foot, turn.

Rep last row, working and joining heel to foot, until 12[13:15] rows and sts have been joined at each side of heel, turn. Cut off C and join in A.

1st round: 3ch (counts as 1htr and 1ch), miss first dc, 1htr into next dc, (1ch, miss next dc, 1htr into next dc) 6[6:7] times, 1ch, miss next dc, 1htr into same st on foot as ss, (1ch, miss next st, 1htr into next st) 13[14:16] times, 1ch, 1htr into same st on foot as ss, 1ch, join with a ss into first sp. 23[24:27] sps.

Cut off A and join in D.

2nd round: 3ch (counts as first tr), leaving last loop of each on hook work 2tr into first sp, yrh and draw through all 3 loops on hook, *1ch, leaving last loop of each on hook work 3tr all into next sp, yrh and draw through all 4 loops on hook (cluster formed), rep from * to end, finishing with 1ch, join with a ss into top of first cluster.

3rd round: 3ch (counts as 1htr and 1ch), 1htr into into first sp, *1ch, 1htr into next sp, rep from * to end, finishing with 1ch, join with a ss into first sp.

4th round: 3ch, leaving last loop of each on hook work 2tr into first sp, yrh and draw through all 3 loops on hook, *1ch, work a cluster into next sp, rep from * to end, finishing with 1ch, join with a ss into top of first cluster.

The last 2 rounds form patt. Joining in and cutting off colours as required, cont in patt in stripes as foll: 1 round A, 3 rounds B, 1 round A, 3 rounds C, 1 round A, 3 rounds D, 1 round A and 3 rounds B. Fasten off.

Sew in ends neatly.

Ruffle scarf

Lacy ruffles are used to create a scarf that has a nostalgic look, although a contemporary colour brings it up to date.

This long lacy scarf is worked in 4-ply yarn and falls into frivolous lacy ruffles, creating a flattering effect while also keeping your neck warm.

The Yarn

Sublime Extra Fine Merino Wool 4-ply (approx. 175m/191 yards per 50g/1¾oz ball) contains 100% merino wool. Spun from the finest-quality fibres, this luxurious yarn can be machine washed at a low temperature. There is a small range of contemporary colours to choose from.

GETTING STARTED

★★ *Pattern is straightforward but working rows along length of scarf needs patience.*

Size:
Finished scarf is approximately 185cm (73in) long when hanging x 10cm (4in) wide when flat

How much yarn:
4 x 50g (1¾oz) balls of Sublime Extra Fine Merino Wool 4-ply in Glamour (shade 130)

Hook:
4.00mm (UK 8) crochet hook

Tension:
1 patt rep measures approximately 5cm (2in) across at outer edge and frill measures approximately 10cm (4in) wide on 4.00mm (UK 8) hook
IT IS ESSENTIAL TO WORK TO THE STATED TENSION TO ACHIEVE SUCCESS

What you have to do:
Make an extra-long foundation chain (to equal length of scarf). Work foundation row in double crochet. Work first side of frill in a lacy pattern, doubling number of stitches on first row to create a ruffle effect. Make picot edging with chain loops along outer edge. Work second side of frill in same way by working into stitches on other side of foundation chain.

Instructions

Abbreviations:
ch = chain(s)
cm = centimetre(s)
dc = double crochet
dtr = double treble
patt = pattern
rem = remain
rep = repeat
sp(s) = space(s)
ss = slip stitch
st(s) = stitch(es)
tr = treble(s)
tr2tog = work 1tr in each of next 2 tr leaving last loop of each on hook, yrh and draw through all 3 loops
yrh = round round hook

SCARF:

With 4.00mm (UK 8) hook make 332ch.

Foundation row: 1dc into 2nd ch from hook, 1dc into each ch to end, turn. 331 sts.

1st row: 5ch (counts as first dtr and 1ch), 1dtr into next st, *1ch, 1dtr into next st, rep from * to end, turn. 331 sts and 330 ch sps.

2nd row: 1ch, 1dc into first st, 2ch, miss next ch sp and st (ie. 2 sts), 1dc into next ch sp or st, *miss next 2 sts, 6tr into next st or ch sp, miss 2 sts, 1dc into next ch sp or st, 2ch, miss 2 sts, 1dc into next st or ch sp, rep from * to end, turn.

3rd row: 1ch, 1dc into first dc, 2ch, *1tr into next tr, (1ch, 1tr into next tr) 5 times, 1dc into next 2ch sp, rep from * to last 2dc omitting 1dc at end of last rep, 2ch, 1dc into last dc, turn.

4th row: 3ch (counts as first tr), (1tr into next tr, 2ch) 5 times, *tr2tog, 2ch, (1tr into next tr, 2ch) 4 times, rep from * to last tr, work 1tr into next tr until 2 loops rem on hook, 1tr into last dc until 3 loops rem on hook, yrh and draw through all 3 loops, turn.

5th row: 1ch, 1dc into first st, 3dc into first 2ch sp, *7ch,

3dc into next 2ch sp, rep from * to last 2tr, 1dc into 3rd of 3ch, do not fasten off but ss along row ends of ruffle to foundation ch, do not turn.

6th row: Work as given for 1st row but working into other side of sts in foundation ch, turn.

7th–10th rows: Work as given for 2nd–5th rows. Fasten off.

Chevron cushion

Here's a great example of how a traditional pattern can be given a modern twist by choosing adventurous colours.

Work chevrons in varying widths and a selection of funky colours for this contemporary cushion. The back is worked in plain trebles, and features a buttoned opening.

The Yarn

Debbie Bliss Rialto DK (approx. 105m/ 114 yards per 50g/1¾oz ball) contains 100% extra fine merino wool. It produces a soft, luxurious fabric, machine-washable at a low temperature. There is a fabulous colour range for contemporary work.

GETTING STARTED

★★ *Chevron pattern is easy to follow, but there are a lot of colour changes.*

Size:

30 x 30cm (12 x 12in)

How much yarn:

1 x 50g (1¾oz) ball of Debbie Bliss Rialto DK in each of five colours: A – Red (shade 12); B – Turquoise (shade 24); C – Orange (shade 32); D – Lime (shade 09) and E – Teal (shade 20)

2 balls in colour F – Bright Pink (shade 34)

Hooks:

3.50mm (UK 9) crochet hook

4.00mm (UK 8) crochet hook

Additional items:

2 x 3.5cm (1⅜in) buttons

30 x 30cm (12 x 12in) cushion pad

33 x 63cm (13 x 25in) rectangle of cotton lining fabric in a toning colour

Matching sewing thread and needle

Tension:

1 patt rep (11 sts) measures 6.5cm (2½in) and 11 rows measure 13cm (5in) over patt on 3.50mm (UK 9) hook

IT IS ESSENTIAL TO WORK TO THE STATED TENSION TO ACHIEVE SUCCESS

What you have to do:

Work cushion front in chevron pattern and stripes. When working stripes, always change to new colour on last part of stitch in old colour. Work cushion backs in trebles throughout and one colour, with borders in double crochet and a contrast colour. Make buttonholes in back border. Sew simple fabric cover for cushion pad so that colour does not show through chevron pattern.

Instructions

Abbreviations:

ch = chain(s)
cm = centimetre(s)
cont = continue
dc = double crochet
dtr = double treble
foll = follows
htr = half treble
patt = pattern
rep = repeat
RS = right side
ss = slip stitch

st(s) = stitch(es)
tog = together
tr = treble(s)
tr2tog = work 1tr into each of next 2 sts leaving last loop of each of hook, yarn round hook and draw through all 3 loops
WS = wrong side

FRONT:

With 4.00mm (UK 8) hook and A, make 57ch. Change to 3.50mm (UK 9) hook.

Foundation row: (RS) 1tr into 4th ch from hook, 1tr into each of next 3ch, *3tr into next ch, 1tr into each of next 4ch, miss next 2ch, 1tr into each of next 4ch, rep from * 3 more times, 3tr into next ch, 1tr into each of last 5ch, turn.

1st row: 3ch (counts as first tr), miss st at base of ch and foll st, 1tr into each of next 4 sts, *3tr into next st, 1tr into each of next 4 sts, miss next 2 sts, 1tr into each of next 4 sts, rep from * 3 more times, 3tr into next st, 1tr into each of next 4 sts, miss next st, 1tr into 3rd of 3ch, turn. The last row forms patt. Cont in patt, working in stripe sequence as foll and always joining in new colour on last part of last st in old colour:
3 more rows A; 2 rows B; 3 rows C; 1 row B; 2 rows D; 3 rows F; 2 rows C; 1 row E; 2 rows D and 4 rows A.

Next row: With F, 3ch (counts as first tr), miss st at base of ch, *tr2tog into next 2 sts, 1htr into next st, 1dc into next st, ss into each of next 3 sts, 1dc into next st, 1htr into next st, tr2tog into next 2 sts, 1dtr into sp between sts, rep from * 3 times more, tr2tog into next 2 sts, 1htr into next st, 1dc into next, ss into each of next 3 sts, 1dc into next st, 1htr into next st, tr2tog into next 2 sts, 1tr into 3rd of 3ch, turn.

Next row: 1ch (does not count as a st), 1dc into each st to end, working last dc into 3rd of 3ch. Fasten off.
Turn Front around and work along other side of foundation ch as foll:
With RS facing, join F to first st, 1ch, 1dc into first st, 1htr into each of next 2 sts, tr2tog into next 2sts, *1tr into next st, tr2tog into next 2 sts, 1htr into each of next 2 sts, 1dc into first of 2ch, 1dc into sp, 1dc into 2nd of 2ch, 1htr into each of next 2 sts, tr2tog into next 2 sts, rep from * 3 more times, 1tr into next st, tr2tog

into next 2 sts, 1htr into each of next 2 sts, 1dc into last st, turn.

Next row: 1ch (does not count as a st), 1dc into each st to end. Fasten off.

LOWER BACK:

With 4.00mm (UK 8) hook and F, make 52ch. Change to 3.50mm (UK 9) hook.

Foundation row: 1tr into 4th ch from hook, 1tr into each ch to end, turn. 50 sts.

1st row: 3ch (counts as first tr), miss st at base of ch, 1tr into each st to end, working last tr into 3rd of 3ch, turn. Work 11 more rows in tr.

Border:

Change to B.

Next row: 1ch (does not count as a st), 1dc into each st to end, working last dc into 3rd of 3ch, turn. Work 3 more rows in dc.

1st buttonhole row: 1ch, 1dc into each of next 16 sts, 3ch, miss next 4 sts, 1dc into each of next 10 sts, 3ch, miss next 4 sts, 1dc into each of next 16 sts, turn.

2nd buttonhole row: Work in dc, working 4dc into each 3ch space, turn.

Work 2 more rows in dc. Fasten off.

TOP BACK:

Work as given for Top back, working 8 rows in dc for border and omitting buttonholes.

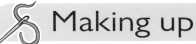 # Making up

Block cushion pieces to shape, lightly spray with clean water and leave until completely dry. Place front WS down on a flat surface and lay lower back in place on top of it, RS down and with buttonhole border in centre. Now lay top back in place, RS down and overlapping borders in centre. Join with a backstitch seam around outer edges. Turn RS out and sew on buttons to correspond with buttonholes.

Cushion lining:

Fold lining fabric in half with RS facing. Taking 1.5cm (⅝in) seam allowances, sew along two adjacent sides, leaving one side open. Turn RS out and press seam allowances along open side to WS. Insert cushion pad and neatly slip stitch seam closed.

Insert covered pad into cover and button closed.

Converter mitts

Keep your fingers covered up or free – the choice is yours with these mitts.

Worked in a subtle felted tweed yarn and ridged double crochet pattern, the button-down top of these mitts folds back to reveal the fingerless mitts underneath.

GETTING STARTED

★ ★ *Easy stitch pattern but lots of details and shaping requires concentration.*

Size:
To fit an average-sized woman's hand

How much yarn:
2 x 50g (1¾oz) balls of Rowan Felted Tweed DK in Watery (shade 152)

Hook:
3.50mm (UK 9) crochet hook

Additional items:
2 small buttons

Tension:
22 sts and 20 rows measure 10cm (4in) square over patt on 3.50mm (UK 9) hook
IT IS ESSENTIAL TO WORK TO THE STATED TENSION TO ACHIEVE SUCCESS

What you have to do:
Work wristband first in mock rib pattern. Pick up stitches for mitt along side edge of wristband and continue in ridged double crochet pattern. Shape for thumb and finger section as directed.

The Yarn
Rowan Felted Tweed DK (approx. 175m/191 yards per 50g/1¾oz ball) contains 50% merino wool, 25% alpaca and 25% viscose. Machine-washable, it makes a soft, matted fabric. It comes in a range of tweed shades.

 Instructions

LEFT MITT:
Wristband:
With 3.50mm (UK 9) hook make 16ch.
Foundation row: (RS) 1dc in 2nd ch from hook, 1dc in each ch to end, turn. 16 sts (counting first ch as 1 st).
1st row: 1ch, miss st at base of ch, 1dcb in each st, ending 1dc in 1ch, turn.
Rep last row 34 more times, ending with a WS row. 36 rows in all. Fasten off.
Main part:
1st round: With RS of wristband facing, rejoin yarn at right of one long edge, 1ch, miss first row, 1dc in side of each of next 35 rows, join into a circle with a ss in first ch. 36 sts.
Patt round: 1ch (counts as first dc), miss st at base of ch, 1dcb in each st to end, join with a ss in first ch.
Shape for thumb:
3rd round: 1ch, miss st at base of ch, 1dcb in each of next 16dch, (2dcb in next dcb) twice, 1dcb in each of next 17dcb, join with a ss in first ch. 38 sts.
4th round: As patt round.
5th round: 1ch, miss st at base of ch, 1dcb in each of next 16dcb, 2dcb in next dcb, 1dcb in each of next 2dcb,

Abbreviations:
alt = alternate
beg = beginning
ch = chain
cm = centimetre(s)
cont = continue
dc = double crochet
dcb = double crochet working into back loop only
dcb2tog = (insert hook in back loop only of next st, yrh and draw a loop through) twice, yrh and draw through all 3 loops
dec = decrease(s)
inc = increas(es)(ing)
patt = pattern
rep = repeat
RS = right side
sp = space
ss = slip stitch
st(s) = stitch(es)
tog = together
WS = wrong side
yrh = yarn round hook

2dcb in next dcb, 1dcb in each of next 17dcb, join with a ss in first ch. 40 sts.
6th round: As patt round.
Cont in this way, inc 2 sts (with 2 extra dcb between incs) on next and every alt round, for a further 8 rounds. 48 sts; 14 rounds from wristband.

Shape thumb hole:
15th round: 1ch, miss st at base of ch, 1dcb in each of next 17dcb, 2ch, miss next 12dcb, 1dcb in each of next 18dcb, join with a ss in first ch.
16th round: 1ch, miss st at base of ch, 1dcb in each of next 17dcb, 1dc in each of 2ch, 1dcb in each of next 18dcb, join with a ss in first ch. 38 sts.
17th–22nd rounds: Patt 6 rounds.

Separate fingers: (Note: next 2 rounds are worked in plain dc not dcb.)
Separating round: 1ch, miss st at base of ch, 1dc in each of next 3dcb, 3ch, 1ss in last dc (picot made), 1dc in each of next 4dcb, 1 picot, 1dc in each of next 5dcb, 1 picot, 1dc in each of next 12dcb, 1dc in tip of last picot made, 1dc in each of next 5dcb, 1dc in tip of second picot made, 1dc in each of next 4dcb, 1dc in tip of first picot made, 1dc in each of next 4dcb, join with a ss in first ch.

Last round: 1ch, miss st at base of ch, 1dc in each of next 3dc, 1dc in right leg of picot, 1ch, 1dc in left leg of picot (1ch sp made), 1dc in each of next 4dc, 1ch sp over next picot, 1dc in each of next 5dc, 1ch sp over next picot, 1dc in each of next 12dc, 1dc in 3rd 1ch sp made, miss dc in tip of picot, 1dc in each of next 5dc, 1dc in 2nd 1ch sp made, miss dc in tip of picot, 1dc in each of next 4dc, 1dc in 1st 1ch sp made, miss dc in tip of picot, 1dc in each of next 4dc, join with a ss in first ch.
Fasten off.

Border for finger section:

With 3.50mm (UK 9) hook make 6ch. Work foundation row as given for Wristband (6 sts), then work 5 rows as given for 1st row of Wristband.

7th row: 6ch, 1dc in 2nd ch from hook, 1dc in each of next 4ch, patt to end, turn. 12 sts.

8th and 9th rows: Work 2 rows in patt.

10th row: 1ch, miss first dcb, 1dcb in each of next 5dcb, 3ch, miss next 3 sts, 1dcb in each of next 2dcb, 1dc in 1ch, turn.

11th row: 1ch, miss first dcb, 1dcb in each of next 2dcb, 1dcb in same place as last st tog with 1dc in 3ch sp, 1dc in 3ch sp, 1dc in 3ch sp tog with 1dcb in next dcb, 1dcb in same place as last insertion, patt to end, turn. 12 sts.

12th and 13th rows: Patt to end.

14th row: 1ch, miss st at base of ch, 1dcb in each of next 5dcb, turn. 6 sts.

Work 5 rows in patt, ending with a RS row. 19 rows in all. Fasten off. *

Finger section:

Rejoin yarn to joining st at beg of last round in dcb (22nd round), below finger separating rounds and work across palm, 1ch, (1dcb in same place as next st of separating round) 18 times, then with RS of flap border facing, work 1dc in side edge of each of 19 rows of unshaped side edge, join with a ss in first ch. 38 sts.

** Work 10 rounds in patt

1st dec round: 1ch, miss st at base of ch, dcb2tog over next 2 sts, 1dcb in each of next 13 sts, dcb2tog over next 2 sts, 1dcb in each of next 2 sts, dcb2tog over next 2 sts, 1dc in each of next 13 sts, dcb2tog over next 2 sts, 1dcb in next st, join with a ss in first ch. 34 sts.

2nd dec round: 1ch, miss st at base of ch, dcb2tog over next 2 sts, 1dcb in each of next 11 sts, dcb2tog over next 2 sts, 1dcb in each of next 2 sts, dcb2tog over next 2 sts, 1dc in each of next 11 sts, dcb2tog over next 2 sts, 1dcb in next st, join with a ss in first ch. 30 sts.

Work 3 more dec rounds in same way, working 2 sts less between 1st and 2nd decs and 3rd and 4th decs, on each round. 18 sts. Fasten off.

Thumb:

With RS of work facing, rejoin yarn at base of first of 2ch made on 15th round.

1st round: 1ch, miss st at base of ch, 1dcb in each of next 12dcb, 1dc in 2nd of 2ch, join with a ss in first ch. 14 sts. Work 10 rounds in patt.

Dec round: 1ch, miss st at base of ch, (dcb2tog) 6 times, 1dcb in last dcb, join with a ss in first ch. Fasten off.

RIGHT MITT:

Work as given for Left mitt to *.

Finger section:

With RS of flap border facing, rejoin yarn at right of long unshaped side edge, 1ch, miss first row, 1dc in side edge of each of next 18 rows, with palm of right mitt facing, 1dcb in each of last 19 sts of last round in dcb (22nd round), join with a ss in first ch. 38 sts.

Complete as given for Left mitt from ** to end.

Making up

Join seam at top of finger section. Sew down short edges of finger section border to straight lines of sts at either side of mitt. Gather top of thumb tightly and secure. Join wristband seam. Sew on button to match buttonhole.

Spiral table mat

Create this stunning centrepiece for your table by crocheting with strips of fabric.

This fabulous table centre is worked in continuous rounds of double crochet from strips of fabric. It has a core of plain calico to give the mat bulk and stability.

The Yarn

This design is based on a rag rug technique and uses strips of fabric instead of yarn. The fabrics can be any old cotton materials (patterned and plain) and they should be washed first. Afterwards the fabrics should be cut into strips as described on page 55.

GETTING STARTED

★★ *Easy stitches but working with strips of fabric requires practice.*

Size:
50cm (20in) in diameter

How much yarn:
1m (1 yard) of calico or old sheeting for the core
Selection of old washed cotton fabrics, including dress materials and shirting

Hook:
8.00mm (UK 0) crochet hook

Additional items:
Needle and sewing thread
Short piece of wool

Tension:
First 6 rounds measure 15cm (6in) in diameter on 8.00mm (UK 0) hook

What you have to do:
Cut up fabrics as directed. Work throughout over strip of core fabric for bulk. Work in continuous rounds of double crochet. Join in new fabrics as required.

Notes:
• You can prepare the fabric first and roll it up into small balls, or cut each piece as you go. Cut a strip approximately 2cm (¾in) wide from one edge of the piece and stop cutting when you are 2cm (¾in) from the far end. Now turn the fabric and start cutting a further 2cm (¾in) down, so that you have one long strip. Continue in this way until the end of the piece of fabric.

• Change colours as you wish during the work. When you need to join in a new length, fold 4cm (1½in) at one end inside the short end of the working length and work one or more stitches with a double thickness to secure the new length.

• For the core, you will need a 5cm (2in) wide strip of calico or old sheeting

Instructions

Abbreviations:
beg = beginning
cm = centimetre(s)
dc = double crochet
st = stitch

TABLE MAT:

Twist first 6cm (2½in) of core fabric into a loop and stitch short end down to secure. Hold loop so that long end lies towards left.

1st round: With 8.00mm (UK 0) hook, fasten on one end of a fabric strip and work 10dc into loop. Do not join into a round, but continue working in a continuous spiral.

2nd round: Working each st over core fabric throughout, work 2dc into each st to end. 20dc. Tie a length of wool to next st to act as a marker for beg of next and subsequent rounds.

3rd round: (1dc into next dc, 2dc into next dc) to end. 30dc.

4th round: 1dc into each dc to end.

5th round: (1dc into each of next 2dc, 2dc into next dc) to end. 40dc.

6th round: 1dc into each dc to end.

7th round: (1dc into each of next 3dc, 2dc into next dc) to end. 50dc.

8th round: (1dc into each of next 4dc, 2dc into next dc) to end. 60dc.

9th round: (1dc into each of next 5dc, 2dc into next dc) to end. 70dc.

10th and 11th rounds: 1dc into each dc to end.

12th round: As 8th. 84dc.

13th round: As 9th. 98dc.

14th round: 1dc into each dc to end.

15th round: (1dc into each of next 6dc, 2dc into next dc) to end. 112dc.

16th round: 1dc into each dc to end.

17th round: (1dc into each of next 7dc, 2dc into next dc) to end. 126dc.

18th round: 1dc into each dc to end.

19th round: (1dc into each of next 8dc, 2dc into next dc) to end. 140dc.

20th and 21st rounds: 1dc into each dc to end.

Fasten off and sew loose end to back of work.

HOW TO
TO CUT THE FABRIC

Old cotton fabric, either plain or patterned, is perfect for this technique. Cut it into strips, roll it into balls, and you're ready to start crocheting this stunning table centrepiece.

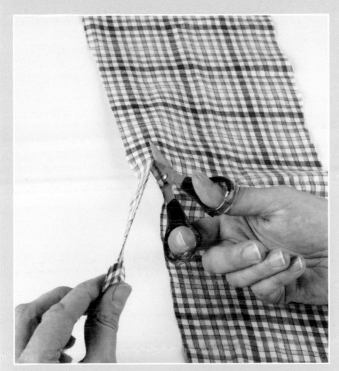

Select a mixture of cotton fabrics with a similar colour palette. They can be patterned, striped, checked or plain. Wash the fabric first and then cut it into strips approximately 2cm (¾in) wide.

2 To make a continuous strip, stop cutting when you are 2cm (¾in) from the end of the piece and turn the fabric. Continue cutting in the opposite direction and repeat this each time you reach the edge of the fabric.

This will give you a long continuous strip of fabric that is 2cm (¾in) wide. Wind each strip up into a small ball. Repeat this with each type of fabric, then you are ready to start work. Change colours as you wish, swapping from ball to ball.

Vertical-striped bag

Stop the traffic on the way to the shops or the beach with this brightly coloured bag.

The front of this bag is worked from side to side in double crochet and bright, zingy stripes separated by a thin black line, while the back and gusset are in different plain colours.

GETTING STARTED

⭐ *Easy double crochet fabric but neat work is required for a professional finish.*

Size:
Bag measures 35cm wide x 38cm high x 8cm deep (14in x 15in x 3in)

How much yarn:
2 x 100g (3½oz) balls of Patons 100% Cotton DK in each of two colours: A – Kingfisher (shade 2379) and D – Cheeky (shade 2719)
1 ball in each of three other colours: B – Grape (shade 2733); C – Nectarine (shade 2723) and E – Black (shade 2712)

Hook:
3.50mm (UK 9) crochet hook

Additional items:
70cm (¾in) of 90cm- (36in-) wide cotton lining fabric
Matching sewing thread and needle
1.5m (1⅝ yard) of 2cm- (¾in-) wide black webbing or ribbon

Tension:
17 sts and 22 rows measure 10cm (4in) square over dc on 3.50mm (UK 9) hook
IT IS ESSENTIAL TO WORK TO THE STATED TENSION TO ACHIEVE SUCCESS

What you have to do:
Work bag front in double crochet and stripe pattern. Work bag back in a plain colour. Make gusset in another plain colour, working directly on to three sides of bag front turned sideways. At end of gusset, crochet directly on to three side of bag back. Work handles and sew in place. Sew fabric lining for bag and strengthen handles with webbing or ribbon.

The Yarn
Patons 100% Cotton DK (approx. 210m/ 229 yards per 100g/3½oz ball) is a pure cotton yarn with a tight twist and subtle sheen. It is machine washable and there are plenty of good shades to use for the colourful stripe combinations.

Instructions

Abbreviations:

beg = beginning
ch = chain(s)
cm = centimetre(s)
cont = continue
dc = double crochet
foll = follows
rep = repeat
RS = right side
st(s) = stitch(es)
WS = wrong side

BAG FRONT:

With 3.50mm (UK 9) hook and A, make 65ch loosely.

Foundation row: (RS) Working into top loop only each time work 1dc into 2nd ch from hook, 1dc into each ch to end, turn. 64 sts.

Next row: 1ch (does not count as a st), 1dc into each dc to end, changing to B on last part of last st, turn. Cont in dc and stripes as foll, always changing to new colour on last part of last st in old colour: 2 rows B, 2 rows C, 2 rows D, 1 row E and 2 rows A. These 9 rows form stripe patt. Rep them until work measures 35cm (14in) from beg. Fasten off.

BAG BACK:

With 3.50mm (UK 9) hook and A, make 65ch loosely.

Foundation row: (RS) Working into top loop only each time work 1dc into 2nd ch from hook, 1dc into each ch to

end, turn. 64 sts.

Next row: 1ch (does not count as a st), 1dc into each dc to end, turn. Cont in dc until work measures 35cm (14in) from beg. Fasten off.

GUSSET:

Turn bag front sideways so that stripes are vertical and foundation ch forms left-hand edge.

With 3.50mm (UK 9) hook and RS of work facing, join D at top left-hand corner and work 64dc down left-hand edge working into back loops of foundation ch, 2dc into corner st, 59dc along row ends of lower edge, 2dc into corner st, then work 64dc up right-hand edge, working into back loops only of sts, turn. 191 sts.

Work in rows of dc until gusset measures 8.5cm (3⅜in) from beg, ending with a RS row.

With RS of both pieces facing, now join gusset to bag back, working through gusset sts and sides and lower edge of back. Fasten off.

HANDLES: (make 2)

With 3.50mm (UK 9) hook and E, make 108ch loosely.

Foundation row: 1dc into 2nd ch from hook, 1dc into each ch to end, turn. 107 sts.

Next row: 1ch (does not count as a st), 1dc into each dc to end, turn.

Work 3 more rows in dc. Fasten off.

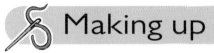

Making up

Sew handles to bag front and back in positions as shown in photograph. Sew webbing or ribbon to underside of handles for extra strength.

Using crochet pieces as a guide, cut front and back pieces and gusset from lining fabric, adding 1.5cm (⅝in) on all edges for seam allowances. Sew lining together in same way as bag. Press under 1.5cm (⅝in) around top edge of lining and place inside bag so that WS of both bag and lining are facing. Slip stitch top edge of lining to underside of top edge of bag.

Bobble hat

This close-fitting hat makes the most of the contrasting textures between the crochet and the furry pompom.

Made in a flecked chunky yarn and textured pattern, this snug-fitting and cosy hat is trimmed with an eye-catching 'furry' pompom.

GETTING STARTED

★★ *Quick to make but working clusters and shaping can be a challenge.*

Size:
To fit an average adult woman's head
Hat measures 58cm (23in) in circumference x 19cm (7½in) deep

How much yarn:
1 x 100g (3½oz) ball of Sirdar Denim Ultra in colour A – Starling (shade 507)
1 x 50g (1¾oz) ball of Sirdar Funky Fur in colour B – Latte (shade 550)

Hooks:
4.00mm (UK 8) crochet hook
5.00mm (UK 6) crochet hook

Additional item:
Piece of cardboard or pompom maker

Tension:
12 sts measure 11cm (4¼in) and 8 rows measure 6.5cm (2½in) over patt using A on 5.00mm (UK 6) hook
IT IS ESSENTIAL TO WORK TO THE STATED TENSION TO ACHIEVE SUCCESS

What you have to do:
Work main pattern in double crochet with clusters on alternating rows. Shape crown by decreasing on double crochet rows. Make pompom in contrast-textured yarn.

The Yarn
Sirdar Denim Ultra (approx. 75m/82 yards per 100g/3½oz ball) is a blend of 60% acrylic, 25% cotton and 15% wool. The finished result resembles denim. There are plenty of denim-look colours to choose from and it can be machine washed. Sirdar Funky Fur (approx. 90m/98 yards per 50g/1¾oz ball) is 100% acyclic. It is a novelty yarn with an eyelash finish that resembles fur. There are plenty of bright shades as well as neutral colours such as this to choose from.

Instructions

Abbreviations:

ch = chain
cm = centimetre(s)
cont = continue
dc = double crochet
dc2(3)tog = into each of next 2(3) sts work: (insert hook into st, yrh and draw a loop through), yrh and draw through all 3(4) loops
foll = follows
patt = pattern
rem = remaining
rep = repeat
st(s) = stitch(es)
tog = together
WS = wrong side
yrh = yarn round hook

HAT:

With 4.00mm (UK 8) hook and A, make 65ch.

Foundation row: 1dc into 2nd ch from hook, 1dc into each ch to end, turn. 64 sts.

Next row: 1ch (does not count as a st), 1dc into each st to end, turn.

Change to 5.00mm (UK 6) hook.

Work 1 more row in dc as before.

Cont in patt as foll:

1st row: (WS) 1ch (does not count as a st), *1dc into each of next 2 sts, work 1 cluster into next st as foll: (yrh, insert hook into st and draw through a loop, yrh and draw through first 2 loops on hook) twice, yrh and draw through all 3 loops on hook, rep from * to last st, 1dc into last st, turn.

2nd row: 1ch, 1dc into next st, *1dc into next cluster, 1dc into each of next 2 sts, rep from * to end, turn.

3rd row: 1ch, 1dc into next st, *1 cluster into next st, 1dc into each of next 2 sts,

rep from * to end, turn.

4th row: 1ch, *1dc into each of next 2 sts, 1dc into next cluster, rep from * to last st, 1dc into last st, turn.

These 4 rows form patt. Rep them once more, then work 1st row again.

Shape crown:

1st row: 1ch, *(dc3tog) twice, 1dc into each of next 6 sts, rep from * to last 4 sts, dc3tog, 1dc into last st, turn. 42 sts.

2nd row: 1ch, *1dc into each of next 2 sts, 1 cluster into next st, rep from * to end, turn.

3rd row: Work in dc.

4th row: 1ch, 1dc into next st, *1 cluster into next st, 1dc into each of next 2 sts, rep from * to last 2 sts, 1 cluster into next st, 1dc into next st, turn.

5th row: 1ch, *dc3tog, 1dc into each of next 6 sts, rep from * to last 6 sts, dc3tog, 1dc into each of next 3 sts, turn. 32 sts.

6th row: 1ch, *1dc into each of next 2 sts, 1 cluster into next st, rep from * to

last 2 sts, 1 dc into each of next 2 sts, turn.
7th row: 1 ch, *dc3tog, 1 dc into each of next 6 sts, rep from * to last 5 sts, dc3tog, 1 dc into each of next 2 sts, turn. 24 sts.
8th row: Work as given for 2nd row of crown shaping.
9th row: *Dc3tog, rep from * to end. 8 sts.
10th row: Work in dc.
11th row: (Dc3tog) twice, dc2tog. 3 sts. Cut off yarn, leaving a long end for joining back seam. Thread yarn through rem sts and fasten off securely.

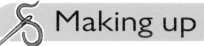

Making up

Join back seam with mattress stitch.
With B, make a pompom 5cm (2in) in diameter. This can be done with a pompom maker. Alternatively, cut two card circles of 5cm (2in) diameter with holes of 2cm (¾in) diameter in the centre. Thread several strands of yarn into a blunt-ended needle and hold the two card rings together. Wind the yarn around the card rings, taking the yarn through the central hole and then around the outer edge. Re-thread the needle as necessary until the central space is filled with yarn. Using sharp scissors cut through the yarn, slipping the blade of the scissors between the two rings and cutting around the edge. Ease the rings apart and tie a length of yarn firmly around the strands in the middle of the rings. Leave the yarn end. Pull the rings apart and off the yarn at each end. Trim off any uneven strands and fluff the pompoms into perfect rounds. Thread the yarn end into the needle and sew the pompom to the centre of the crown.

Chic felted bag

This is a really cool little bag in subtle stripes with a button fastening. It will take pride of place in your wardrobe.

In an array of colours made subtle by felting, this shoulder bag with a button fastening is a simple and stylish accessory.

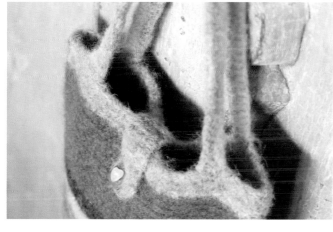

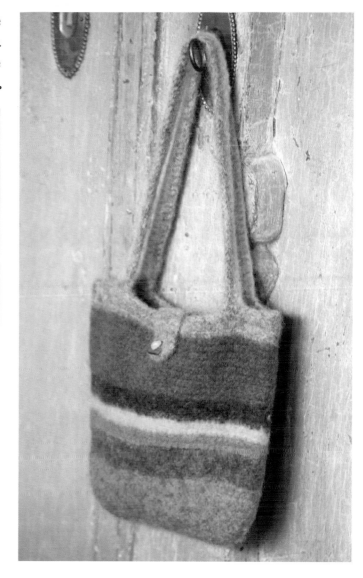

The Yarn
Jamieson & Smith 2-Ply Jumper Weight yarn (approx. 114m/125 yards per 25g/1oz ball) is 100% Shetland wool and is equivalent to a 4-ply yarn. It is traditionally used for knitting Fair Isle garments and there is a large colour palette to choose from.

GETTING STARTED

 Easy to work in a basic fabric but you will need to be confident with felting.

Size:
Finished bag is approximately 20cm (8in) wide x 19cm (7½in) high x 4cm (1½in) deep

How much yarn:
1 x 25g (1oz) ball of Jamieson & Smith 2-Ply Jumper Weight yarn in each of seven colours: A – Pumpkin (shade 91); B – Russet (shade 9144); C – Moss (shade FC44); D – Buttermilk (shade 66); E – Heather (shade FC55); F – Hazel (shade 120) and G – Periwinkle (shade FC15)

Hook:
4.00mm (UK 8) crochet hook

Additional items:
2 buttons (1 large and 1 smaller)
White sewing thread and needle

Tension:
Work to your usual tension as accuracy is not necessary as the fabric will be felted

What you have to do:
Work in double crochet and coloured stripes throughout. Work around foundation chain, increasing at sides to create base of bag. Continue straight in rounds of double crochet. Incorporate handles into top edge of bag. Make buttonhole flap to close top edge. Felt finished bag in a washing machine.

Instructions

Abbreviations:

ch = chain(s)

cm = centimetre(s)

cont = continue

dc = double crochet

foll = follows

rep = repeat

RS = right side

ss = slip stitch

st(s) = stitch(es)

Note:

Yarn is used double throughout

BAG:

With 4.00mm (UK 8) hook and 2 strands of A, make 32ch.

Foundation round: 3dc into 2nd ch from hook (mark 2nd of these 3dc), 1dc into each ch to last ch, 3dc into last ch (mark 2nd of these 3dc), then work 1dc into each st along other side of foundation ch, join with a ss into first dc. 64 sts.

1st round: 2ch (counts as first dc), miss first st, 1dc into each st in previous round, working 3dc into marked centre st at either side, join with a ss into 2nd of 2ch. 68 sts.

Rep last round 3 times more to create base of bag. 80 sts.

Next round: 2ch, miss first st, 1dc into each st to end, join with a ss into 2nd of 2ch.

Rep last round 5 times more.

Cut off A and join in B.

Work 5 rounds in B. Cut off B and join in C.

Work 2 rounds in C. Cut off C and join in D. Work 2 rounds in D. Cut off D and join in E. Work 3 rounds in E. Cut off E and join in F. Work 9 rounds in F. Cut off F and join in G. Work 3 rounds in G.

Work border and handles:

Next round: Cont in G, 2ch, miss first st, 1dc into each of next 9 sts, 80ch, miss next 20 sts of previous round, 1dc into each of next 20 sts, 80ch, miss next 20 sts of previous round, 1dc into each of next 10 sts, join with a ss into 2nd of 2ch.

Next round: 2ch, miss first st, 1dc into each st to end (working around top of bag and into ch loops for handles), join with a ss into 2nd of 2ch. Fasten off.

Handle edging:

With RS of top edge facing, join D in 2nd st from base of one handle, 1dc into first st of handle, 1dc into each st around handle, miss next st on top edge of bag, ss into next st. Fasten off.

Work second handle in same way.

Buttonhole flap:

Lay bag flat and count 7 sts from inside edge of one of handles (bag back), rejoin G to this st and cont as foll:

Foundation row: 2ch (counts as first

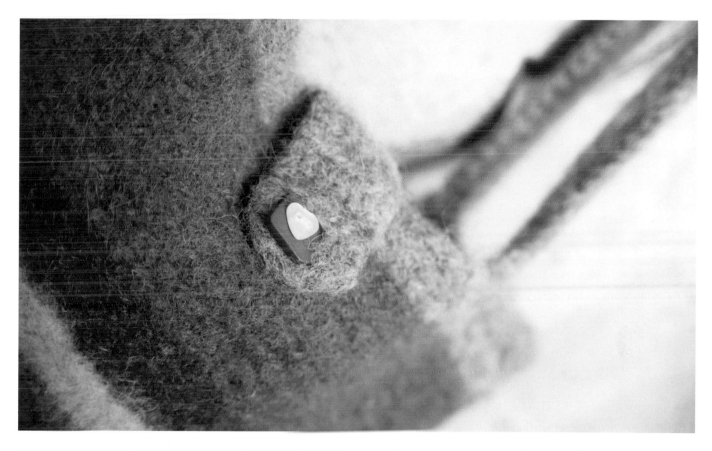

dc), 1dc into each of next 6 sts, turn. 7 sts.

1st row: 2ch, miss first st, 1dc into each st to end, turn.
Rep last row 8 times more.

Next row: (buttonhole) 2ch, miss first st, 1dc into next
st, 4ch, miss next 3 sts, 1dc into next st, 1dc into 2nd of
2ch, turn.

Next row: Ss into each st to end. Fasten off.

Making up

To felt, machine wash at 40°C with normal washing
powder; do not use conditioner and do not spin.
Squeeze out excess water, pull bag gently into shape
and lay out flat to dry.
Using smaller button on top of large one, sew button on
to bag front to correspond with buttonhole on flap.

Matching hat and scarf

Beat the chill in this cosy combination of pull-on hat and short scarf.

This complementary set of hat and matching scarf is worked in a beautiful alpaca yarn. The plain, wide treble pattern throughout is off-set with attractive details in a toning colour – a looped edging on the scarf and staggered stripes on the hat.

The Yarn

Artesano Alpaca DK (approx. 100m/109 yards per 50g/1¾oz ball) contains pure superfine alpaca. It is a soft luxurious yarn in a double knitting weight. Handwash only, there are plenty of neutral and colourful shades.

GETTING STARTED

★★ *Easy fabric for scarf and hat but decorative touches require practice.*

Size:
Scarf: 18cm (7in) wide x 100cm (40in) long (excluding edging)
Hat: 56cm (22in) circumference

How much yarn:
Scarf: 3 x 50g (1¾oz) balls of Artesano 100% Alpaca DK in colour A – Bolivia (shade 0785)
1 ball in colour B – Anemone (shade C986)
Hat: 2 x 50g (1¾oz) balls of Artesano 100% Alpaca DK in colour A – Bolivia (shade 0785)
1 ball in colour B – Anemone (shade C986)
Note: Set takes 4 balls A and 1 ball B

Hook:
4.00mm (UK 8) crochet hook

Tension:
16 sts and 10 rows measure 10cm (4in) square over wide tr patt on 4.00mm (UK 8) hook
IT IS ESSENTIAL TO WORK TO THE STATED TENSION TO ACHIEVE SUCCESS

What you have to do:
Work main section of scarf in wide treble pattern. Work pendant edging at ends in contrast colour. Work crown of hat in wide treble pattern increasing as instructed. Work straight for sides, adding contrast-colour stripes. Work surface crochet over final rounds.

Instructions

Abbreviations:

ch = chain
cm = centimetre(s)
cont = continue
dc = double crochet
foll = follows
htr = half treble
patt = pattern
rep = repeat
RS = right side
sp(s) = space(s)
ss = slip stitch
st(s) = stitch(es)
tr = treble
trb = inserting hook from back and from right to left, work 1tr around stem of next tr
WS = wrong side
yrh = yarn round hook

SCARF:

With 4.00mm (UK 8) hook and A, make 29ch loosely.

1st row: (WS) 1tr in 4th ch from hook, 1tr in each ch to end, turn. 27 sts.

Cont in wide tr patt working into sps between sts as foll:

Patt row: 2ch, *1tr in sp before next tr, rep from * ending 1tr in sp before turning ch, turn.

Rep patt row until work measures 100cm (40in), ending with a WS row. Fasten off.

Pendant edging:

With RS facing, join B in sp between 1st and 2nd sts of last row, 1ch, 1dc in same place, 12ch, ss in 3rd ch from dc to form a ring, (1dc, 1htr, 12tr, 1htr, 1dc) in ring, ss in same ch as last ss – pendant worked, 3ch, miss 4 sps of last row, 1dc in next sp, *12ch, ss in 3rd ch from dc to form a ring, (1dc, 1htr and 1tr) in ring, drop loop

from hook, insert hook in 11th of 12tr of last pendant, replace loop on hook and pull through 11th of 12tr, now work (11tr, 1htr and 1dc) in same ring, ss in same ch as last ss – pendant worked, 3ch, miss 4 sps of last row, 1dc in next sp, rep from * 3 times.

Fasten off.

Work pendant edging along other end.

HAT:
Crown:

1st round: With 4.00mm (UK 8) hook and A, make 4ch, 9tr in 4th ch from hook, ss in 3rd of 3ch. 10 sts.

Cont in wide tr patt working into sps between sts as foll:

2nd round: 2ch, 1tr in first sp, (2tr in next sp) 9 times, ss in 2nd of 2ch. 20 sts.

3rd round: 2ch, 1tr in first sp, 1tr in next sp, (2tr in next sp, 1tr in next sp) 9 times,

ss in 2nd of 2ch. 30 sts.

4th round: 2ch, 1tr in first sp, 1tr in each of next 2 sps, (2tr in next sp, 1tr in each of next 2 sps) 9 times, ss in 2nd of 2ch. 40 sts.

5th round: 2ch, 1tr in first sp, 1tr in each of next 3 sps, (2tr in next sp, 1tr in each of next 3 sps) 9 times, ss in 2nd of 2ch. 50 sts.

6th round: 2ch, 1tr in first sp, 1tr in each of next 4 sps, (2tr in next sp, 1tr in each of next 4 sps) 9 times, ss in 2nd of 2ch. 60 sts.

7th round: 2ch, 1tr in first sp, 1tr in each of next 5 sps, (2tr in next sp, 1tr in each of next 5 sps) 9 times, ss in 2nd of 2ch. 70 sts.

8th round: 2ch, 1trb around stem of each tr, ss in 2nd of 2ch.

Sides:

9th round: 2ch, 1tr in first sp, 1tr in each of next 6 sps, (2tr in next sp, 1tr in each of next 6 sps) 9 times, ss in 2nd of 2ch. 80 sts.

10th round: 2ch, 1tr in first sp, 1tr in each of next 7 sps, (2tr in next sp, 1tr in each of next 7 sps) 9 times, ss in 2nd of 2ch. 90 sts.

11th round: 2ch, 1tr in first sp, 1tr in each sp to last sp, miss last sp, ss in 2nd of 2ch.

12th–17th rounds. As 11th round. Do not fasten off, but carry yarn loosely up back of work. Join in B.

18th round: With B, as 11th round.

19th round: With A, as 11th round.

20th round: With B, as 11th round.

21st–23rd rounds: With A, as 11th round.

Surface crochet:

Take care to work surface crochet at same tension as Hat. Turn Hat 90° so that rounds are vertical, not horizontal. Instead of working from right to left, work up last round as foll: hold A on WS, insert hook into first sp between sts, yrh and draw loop through to RS, *insert hook through next sp between sts, yrh and draw loop through to RS and through loop on hook, rep from * to end. Fasten off.

With A, work a row of surface crochet on next round of wide tr patt. Miss next round. With B, work a row of surface crochet on 18th and 20th rounds.

Fasten off.

Fruity egg cosies

Bring a smile to your breakfast table (and keep your eggs warm) with these funky egg cosies.

Make your breakfast eggs twice the fun with this collection of fabulous cosies based on fruit, and worked in a variety of stitch patterns for a jolly appearance.

GETTING STARTED

★★★ *Cosies may be small but they contain several textured stitch patterns and lots of shaping.*

Size:
Each cosy measures approximately 5–6cm (2–2½in) in diameter x 9–10cm (3½–4in) tall

How much yarn:
1 x 50g (1¾oz) ball of Rowan Pure Wool DK in each of six colours: A – Kiss (shade 036); B – Emerald (shade 022); C – Gilt (shade 032); D – Damson (shade 030); E – Earth (shade 018); F – Avocado (shade 019)

Hook:
4.00mm (UK 8) crochet hook

Additional items:
Stitch markers
Approximately 36 yellow or gold seed beads
Red sewing thread and beading needle

Tension:
Strawberry – 12 sts and 10 rows; pineapple – 12 sts and 8 rows; blackberry – 9 sts and 6 rows; pear – 13 sts and 14 rows all measure 6cm square over patt on 4.00mm (UK 8) hook
IT IS ESSENTIAL TO WORK TO THE STATED TENSION TO ACHIEVE SUCCESS

What you have to do:
Work each cosy in the round in stitch pattern and shaping as described. Make separate leaves and stalks and sew to top of cosies. Decorate strawberry cosy with sew-on bead 'seeds'.

The Yarn
Rowan Pure Wool DK contains 100% wool in a superwash format, which is ideal for these cosies. There is a wide range of beautiful colours to choose from.

 Instructions

STRAWBERRY COSY:
(Worked with WS facing)
With 4.00mm (UK 8) hook, make a magic circle as foll: Wind A several times around tip of left forefinger. Carefully slip ring off finger, insert hook into ring, pull yarn through and make 1ch, then work 7dc in ring, join with a ss in first dc. Pull end of yarn gently to close ring. 7 sts. Marking beg of each round, cont as foll:
1st round: 2dc in each st to end. 14 sts. *
2nd round: (2dc in next st, 1dc in next st) to end. 21 sts.
3rd round: (2dc in next st, 1dc in each of next 2 sts) to end. 28 sts.
4th round: 1dc in each st to end.
5th round: (2dc in next st, 1dc in each of next 3 sts) to end. 35 sts. **
6th round: 1tr in next st, (1dc in next st, 1tr in next st) to end.

Abbreviations:

beg = beginning
ch = chain(s)
cm = centimetre(s)
cont = continue
dc = double crochet
dc2(3)tog = (insert hook into next st and draw a loop through) 2(3) times, yrh and draw through all 3(4) loops
dtr = double treble
dtr3tog = work 3dtr in same st leaving last loop of each on hook, yrh and draw through all 4 loops
foll = follows
htr = half treble
htr3tog = (yrh, insert hook in next st, yrh and draw loop through) 3 times, yrh and draw through all 7 loops
rem = remaining
rep = repeat
RS = right side
sp = space
ss = slip stitch
st(s) = stitch(es)
tr = treble
tr2tog = work 1tr into each of next 2 sts leaving last loop of each on hook, yrh and draw through all 3 loops
WS = wrong side
yrh = yarn round hook
4(5) st bobble = work 4(5)tr in same st leaving last loop of each on hook, yrh and draw through all 5(6) loops

7th round: 1dc in next st, (1tr in next st, 1dc in next st) to end.

8th–15th rounds: Rep 6th and 7th rounds 4 times.

16th round: (Miss next st, 3tr in next st, miss next st, ss in next st) to end. Fasten off. Turn to RS.

Stalk and leaves:

(Worked with WS facing)
With 4.00mm (UK 8) hook and B, make a magic circle (see page 73), 1ch, work 4dc in ring, join with a ss in first dc. Pull end of yarn gently to close ring. 4 sts.
Marking beg of each round, cont as foll: Work 4 rounds in dc on these 4 sts.
Next round: 1dc in first dc, (2dc in next dc) 3 times. 7 sts.
Next round: (1ch, 1dc in next dc) 7 times.
Next round: (Ss in 1ch sp of stalk, 7ch, miss 1ch, ss in each of next 2ch, 1dc in each of next 2ch, 1tr in each of last 2ch, ss in next dc on stalk) 7 times. Fasten off, leaving a long end.

PINEAPPLE COSY:

Using C instead of A, work as given for Strawberry cosy to **.
6th round: (WS) (Miss 2 sts, 5tr – called 1 shell – in next st, miss 2 sts, ss in next st) 5 times, miss 2 sts, 1 shell in next st, miss next st, ss in next st. 6 shells.
7th round: 3ch (counts as first tr), 4tr in ss at base of ch, ss in centre tr of next shell, (1 shell in next ss, ss in centre tr of next shell) 5 times, join with a ss in 3rd of 3ch, turn.
8th–15th rounds: (Ss, 3ch, 4tr) in ss at end of last round, (ss in centre tr of

next shell, 1 shell in next ss) 5 times, ss in centre tr of last shell, join with a ss in 3rd of 3ch, turn. Fasten off. Turn to RS.
Leaf: (make 7)
With 4.00mm (UK 8) hook and B, make 14ch. Working into foundation ch, cont as foll: miss 1ch, htr3tog over next 3ch, 1dc in each of next 5ch, ss in each of next 5ch, then cont along other side of foundation ch as foll: ss in each of next 5ch, 1dc in each of next 5ch, htr3tog over next 3ch, join with a ss in top of first htr3tog. Fasten off, leaving a long end on one leaf only (weave in other ends neatly).

BLACKBERRY COSY:

(Worked with WS facing)
Using D instead of A, work as given for Strawberry cosy to **.
6th round: 3ch (counts as first tr), 1tr in st at base of ch, (5-st bobble in next st, 1tr in each of next 2 sts) to last st, 5-st bobble in last st, join with a ss in 3rd of 3ch.
7th round: 3ch, miss st at base of ch, (5-st bobble in next st, 1tr in each of next 2 sts) to last 2 sts, 5-st bobble in next st, 1tr in last st, join with a ss in 3rd of 3ch.
8th round: 3ch, 4-st bobble in st at base of ch, (1tr in each of next 2 sts, 5-st bobble in next st) to last 2 sts, 1tr in each of last 2 sts, join with a ss in top of first bobble.
9th round: 3ch, miss st at base of ch, 1tr in next st, (5-st bobble in next st, 1tr in each of next 2 sts) to last st, 5-st bobble in last st, join with a ss in 3rd of 3ch.
10th round: 3ch, miss st at base of ch,

(5 st bobble in next st, tr2tog over next 2 sts, 5-st bobble in next st, 1 tr in each of next 2 sts) 5 times, 5-st bobble in next st, tr2tog over next 2 sts, 5-st bobble in next st, 1 tr in last st, join with a ss in 3rd of 3ch. 30 sts.

11th round: 3ch, 4-st bobble in st at base of ch, (1 tr in next tr, 5-st bobble in next st, 1 tr in each of next 2tr, 5-st bobble in next st) 5 times, 1 tr in next tr, 5-st bobble in next st, 1 tr in each of next 2tr, join with a ss in top of first bobble.

12th round: 3ch, miss st at base of ch, (5-st bobble in next st, tr2tog over next 2 sts, 5-st bobble in next st, 1 tr in next st) 5 times, 5-st bobble in next st, tr2tog over next 2 sts, 5-st bobble in last st, join with a ss in 3rd of 3ch. 24 sts.

13th round: 1ch, 1dc in each st, join with a ss to first dc. Fasten off. Turn to RS.

Leaf rosette:
With B, work as given for Strawberry cosy to *.

Next round: (5ch, dtr3tog in next st, 3ch, ss in next st) to end, join with a ss in first of 5ch. Fasten off, leaving a long end.

Stalk:
With 4.00mm (UK 8) hook and E, make a magic circle (see page 73), 1ch, work 4dc in ring, join with a ss in first dc. Pull end of yarn gently to close ring. 4 sts.
Marking beg of each round, cont as foll:
Work 4 rounds in dc on these 4 sts. Fasten off, leaving a long end.

PEAR COSY:
(Worked with WS facing)
With F, work as given for Strawberry cosy to *.
2nd–4th rounds: 1dc in each st to end.

5th round: (2dc in next st, 1dc in next st) to end. 21 sts.
6th round: 1dc in each st to end.
7th round: (2dc in next st, 1dc in each of next 2 sts) to end. 28 sts.
8th and 9th rounds: 1dc in each st to end.
10th round: (2dc in next st, 1dc in each of next 3 sts) to end. 35 sts.
11th–22nd rounds: 1dc in each st to end.
23rd round: 1ch, ss in each st to end. Fasten off. Turn to RS.

Leaf:
(Worked with WS facing)
With 4.00mm (UK 8) hook and B, make 8ch. Miss 1ch, ss in each of next 2ch, 1dc in each of next 2ch, 1htr in each of next 2ch, 6htr in last ch, then cont along other side of foundation ch as foll: 1htr in each of next 2ch, 1dc in each of next 2ch, ss in each of last 2ch. Fasten off, leaving a long end. Thread end into a yarn needle and working running sts down centre of leaf from tip to base, ready for attaching to pear.

Stalk:
Work as given for Stalk of Blackberry cosy.

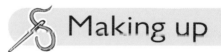

Making up

STRAWBERRY COSY:
Using long end, sew stalk and leaves to top of strawberry, leaving ends of leaves free. Sew on beads in rows as shown in picture, alternating their position on each row.

PINEAPPLE COSY:
Take 4 leaves (one with long tail, threaded into yarn needle) and sew together in cross shape with wide ends in centre. Rep with rem 3 leaves, evenly spacing points, then sew 3 leaves on top of 4 leaves. Sew securely to top of cosy.

BLACKBERRY COSY:
Using long end, sew stalk to centre of leaf rosette, finishing ends underneath. Sew leaf rosette firmly to top of blackberry, with anchor sts between each leaf.

PEAR COSY:
Sew leaf to one side of central hole in top of pear and fasten off inside cosy. Sew stalk to top of cosy, at one side of leaf and covering hole.

Two-colour fingerless mitts

Team soft cream with brown yarn to make these cosy fingerless mitts.

These long mitts are worked mainly in double crochet in a soft luxurious yarn and change colour at the wrist with a decorative band of openwork pattern.

The Yarn

Rowan Baby Alpaca DK (approx. 100m/109 yards per 50g/1¾oz ball) contains 100% baby alpaca. It produces a luxurious fabric that is handwash only. There is a good colour palette including subtle natural shades and some deep colours.

GETTING STARTED

Simple project to practise working in rounds; thumb and finger shaping takes concentration.

Size:

To fit an average woman's hand; width around palm, 18cm (7in)

How much yarn:

2 x 50g (1¾oz) balls of Rowan Baby Alpaca DK in each of two colours: A – Cheviot (shade 207) and B – Jacob (shade 205)

Hook:

4.00mm (UK 8) crochet hook

Tension:

18 sts and 24 rows measure 10cm (4in) square over dc on 4.00mm (UK 8) hook
IT IS ESSENTIAL TO WORK TO THE STATED TENSION TO ACHIEVE SUCCESS

What you have to do:

Work cuff section in first colour and rounds of double crochet. Change to second colour at wrist and work a decorative band of trebles and chain spaces. Continue hand in rounds of double crochet, shaping for thumb and fingers as instructed. Work frill along foundation edge of cuffs.

Instructions

Abbreviations:
beg = beginning
ch = chain
cm = centimetre(s)
cont = continue
dc = double crochet
foll = follow(s)(ing)
inc = increase
patt = pattern
rep = repeat
RS = right side
sp = space
ss = slip stitch
st(s) = stitch(es)
tr = treble
WS = wrong side

RIGHT MITT:
With 4.00mm (UK 8) hook and A, make 35ch.
Foundation round: 1dc into 2nd ch from hook, 1dc into each ch to end, join with a ss into first dc, turn. 34 sts.
Working in rounds but turning work at end of each round, cont as foll:
Patt round: 1dc into each st to end, join with a ss into first dc, turn.
Rep last round until work measures 11cm (4¼in) from beg. Fasten off A and join in B to same place. Cont in B only, work wristband as foll:
1st round: 4ch (counts as 1tr and 1ch), miss st at base of ch and foll st, 1tr into next st, *1ch, miss next st, 1tr into next st, rep from * to end, finishing 1ch, miss next st, join with a ss into 3rd of 4ch, turn.
2nd round: 3ch (counts as first tr), 1tr into first sp, *1tr into next tr, 1tr into next sp, rep from * to end, join with a ss into 3rd of 3ch, turn.
3rd round: As 1st round.
4th round: 1dc into first sp, 1dc into next tr, *1dc into next sp, 1dc into next tr, rep from * to end, join with a ss into first dc, turn. 34 sts.
Cont in dc until work measures 10cm (4in) from beg of wristband.
1st thumb round: (RS) 1dc into first dc, 8ch, miss next 8 sts for thumb opening, patt to end, join with a ss into first dc, turn.
2nd thumb round: 1dc into each of

next 25 sts, 1dc into each of next 8ch, 1dc into last st, join with a ss into first dc, turn. 34 sts.

Cont in patt until work measures 4cm (1½in) from beg of thumb opening, ending with a WS row.

First finger:

Next round: (RS) 1dc into each of first 4 sts, 2dc into next st, miss next 24 sts, 2dc into next st, 1dc into each of last 4 sts, join with a ss into first dc, turn. 12 sts.

Patt 6 rounds on these 12 sts. Fasten off.

Second finger:

With RS facing, join B to same st as first inc on first finger, 1ch (counts as first dc), 1dc into each of next 4 sts, 2dc into next st, miss next 14 sts, 2dc into next st, 1dc into each of next 4 sts, 1dc into same dc as second inc on first finger, join with a ss into first ch, turn. 14 sts.

Patt 8 rounds on these 14 sts. Fasten off.

Third finger:

With RS facing, join B to same st as first inc on second finger, 1ch, 1dc into each of next 3 sts, 2dc into next st, miss next 6 sts, 2dc into next st, 1dc into each of next 3 sts, 1dc into same dc as second inc on second finger, join with a ss into first ch, turn. 12 sts.

Patt 6 rounds on these 14 sts. Fasten off.

Fourth finger:

With RS facing, join B to same st as first inc on third

finger, 1ch, 1dc into same st, 1dc into each of next 6 sts, 2dc into same st as second inc on third finger, join with a ss into first ch, turn. 10 sts.

Patt 4 rounds on these 10 sts. Fasten off.

Thumb:

With RS facing, join B to first st at thumb opening and work 1ch (counts as first dc), 1dc into each st and 1dc into each ch around opening, join with a ss into first ch. 16 sts.

Patt 6 rounds on these 16 sts. Fasten off.

Frill:

With 4.00mm (UK 8) hook and RS of work facing, join A to first foundation ch and work 3ch (counts as first tr), 3tr into first ch, 4tr into each ch to end, join with a ss into 3rd of 3ch. Fasten off.

LEFT MITT:

Work as given for Right mitt but working 2 thumb rounds as foll:

1st thumb round: (RS) 1dc into each of first 25 sts, 8ch, miss next 8 sts for thumb opening, 1dc into last st, join with a ss into first dc, turn.

2nd thumb round: 1dc into first st, 1dc into each of next 8ch, 1dc into each st to end, join with a ss into first dc, turn. 34 sts.

Cable hot-water bottle cover

This cabled cover looks and feels wonderfully cosy.

Worked in a soft alpaca and silk yarn with a textured cable and rib pattern, this hot-water bottle cover is ideal to cuddle up with on a cold night.

GETTING STARTED

★★ *Not much shaping involved but working cable pattern requires concentration.*

Size:
To fit a standard hot-water bottle, 20 x 35cm (8 x 14in)

How much yarn:
4 x 50g (1¾oz) balls of Debbie Bliss Andes in Pale Blue (shade 11)

Hook:
4.00mm (UK 8) crochet hook

Additional items:
3 buttons, 2cm (¾in) in diameter
Piece of cardboard or pompom maker

Tension:
19 sts and 13 rows measure 10cm (4in) square over patt on 4.00mm (UK 8) hook
IT IS ESSENTIAL TO WORK TO THE STATED TENSION TO ACHIEVE SUCCESS

What you have to do:
Work in cable pattern with relief trebles throughout, making buttonhole band in double crochet. Work mock ribbing with relief trebles for top of cover. Make a twisted cord and trim with pompoms to tie around neck of cover.

The Yarn
Debbie Bliss Andes (approx. 100m/109 yards per 50g/1¾oz ball) is a blend of 65% baby alpaca and 35% mulberry silk. It produces a luxurious soft, silky fabric. It is handwash only. There is a good range of colours.

Instructions

Abbreviations:

beg = beginning
ch = chain(s)
cm = centimetre(s)
cont = continue
cross 6 = miss next 3 sts,
work 1rtrf around stem
of each of next 3 sts, now
working in front of last
3 sts work 1rtrf around
stems of 3 missed sts,
beg at original first st
dc = double crochet
foll = follows
patt = pattern
rep = repeat
rtrb = relief tr back as
foll: yrh, insert hook
from back and from right
to left around stem of
next st, yrh and draw a
loop through, complete
tr in usual way
rtrf = relief tr front as
foll: yrh, insert hook from
front and from right to
left around stem of next
st, yrh and draw a loop
through, complete tr in
usual way **sp** = space
ss = slip stitch
st(s) = stitch(es)
tr = treble
tr2tog = (yrh, insert hook
into next st and draw a
loop through, yrh and
draw through first two
loops on hook) twice, yrh
and draw through all 3
loops on hook
yrh = yarn round hook

LOWER FRONT FLAP AND BACK: (Worked in one piece)

With 4.00mm (UK 8) hook make 39ch.

Buttonhole band:

1st row: (RS) 1dc into 2nd ch from hook, 1dc in each ch to end, turn. 38 sts.
2nd row: 1ch (does not count as a st), 1dc in each of first 8 sts, (2ch, miss 2 sts, 1dc in each of next 8 sts) 3 times, turn.
3rd row: 1ch, 1dc in each st and 2dc in each 2ch sp to end, turn.

4th row: 3ch (counts as first tr), miss st at base of ch, 1tr in each st to end, turn. Cont in cable patt as foll:

1st row: (RS) 2ch (counts as first tr), miss st at base of ch, 1tr in next st, 1rtrf around stem of next st, 1tr in each of next 2 sts, (1rtrf around stem of next 6 sts, 1tr in each of next 2 sts, 1rtrf around stem of next st, 1tr in each of next 2 sts) 3 times, working last tr in top of turning ch, turn.

2nd row: 2ch, miss st at base of ch, 1tr in next st, 1rtrb around stem of next st, 1tr in each of next 2 sts, (1rtrb around stem of next 6 sts, 1tr in each of next 2 sts, 1rtrb around stem of next st, 1tr in each of next 2 sts) 3 times, working last tr in top of turning ch, turn.

3rd and 4th rows: As 1st and 2nd rows.

5th row: 2ch, miss st at base of ch, 1tr in next st, 1rtrf around stem of next st, 1tr in each of next 2 sts, (cross 6, 1tr in each of next 2 sts, 1rtrf around stem of next st, 1tr in each of next 2 sts) 3 times, working last tr in top of turning ch, turn.

6th row: As 2nd row, taking care to work 6 crossed sts in their new order. Insert markers at each end of last row to denote lower back edge of cover. The last 6 rows form patt. Rep them 5 times more, then work 1st and 2nd rows again.

Shape top:
Next row: 2ch, miss st at base of ch, tr2tog over next 2 sts, patt to last 3 sts, tr2tog over next 2 sts, 1tr in top of turning ch, turn.
Rep last row 3 times more. 30 sts. Fasten off.

FRONT:
With 4.00mm (UK 8) hook make 39ch.
1st row: (RS) 1dc in 2nd ch from hook, 1dc in each ch to end, turn. 38 sts.
2nd and 3rd rows: 1ch (does not count as a st), 1dc in each st to end, turn.

4th row: 3ch (counts as first tr), miss st at base of ch, 1tr in each st to end, turn. Cont in cable patt as given for Lower front flap and back until 32 rows have been worked.
Shape top:
Work as given for Lower front flap and back, but do not fasten off.
Next row: Ss in each of next 6 sts, do not fasten off but leave on one side for working ribbing.

Making up

Ribbing:
With RS facing, join shaped seams at top for both pieces and 6 sts at either side of top edge. With yarn left at end of Front, work in rib patt around top edge as foll:
Next round: 2ch (does not count as a st), (1rtrf around stem of next st, 1rtrb around stem of next st) 9 times across centre front and 9 times across centre back, join with a ss in first rtrf. 36 sts. Rep last round until ribbing measures 7cm (2¾in) from beg. Fasten off.
With RS of both pieces facing, join side seams, folding back along marked edge so that lower front flap is under main piece of front. Turn RS out and sew on buttons to correspond with buttonholes.
Make a twisted cord approximately 90cm (35in) long and sew centre of cord to centre back of cover at base of ribbing. Make two pompoms (see Making Up instructions on page 63) and sew one to each end of cord. Tie cord in a neat bow around neck of cover.

Crochet hook roll

Have all sizes of crochet hook to hand with this practical roll-up case.

Keep your crochet hooks handy in this easy-to-make crochet case worked in a variegated yarn with a fabric lining. Just roll the case up and secure with crochet ties decorated with flower motifs.

GETTING STARTED

★ ★ *Crocheted main piece is very easy but simple sewing skills are necessary for lining the project.*

Size:
Case measures approximately 25cm (10in) wide x 22cm (8½in) high when unrolled

How much yarn:
1 x 100g (3½oz) ball of King Cole Mirage DK in colour A – Nice (shade 873)
1 x 100g (3½oz) ball of King Cole Haze DK in colour B – Damson (shade 456)

Hooks:
3.50mm (UK 9) crochet hook
4.00mm (UK 8) crochet hook

Additional items:
80 x 25cm (32 x 10in) rectangle of cotton lining fabric
Matching sewing thread

Tension:
17 sts and 14 rows measure 10cm (4in) square over htr on 4.00mm (UK 8) hook
IT IS ESSENTIAL TO WORK TO THE STATED TENSION TO ACHIEVE SUCCESS

What you have to do:
Work main piece in half trebles in variegated yarn. Work edging around main piece in double crochet and solid-coloured yarn. Make chain and slip-stitch ties decorated with flower motifs. Sew separate fabric lining with pockets for hooks. Stitch lining on top of crochet main piece.

The Yarn
King Cole Mirage DK (approx. 312m/340 yards per 100g/3½oz ball) is 50% wool and 50% acrylic and there is a good range of variegated colours. Use solid-coloured King Cole Haze DK (approx. 488m/532 yards per 100g/3½oz ball) – a brushed 100% acrylic yarn – for the edgings and ties.

Instructions

Abbreviations:

beg = beginning
ch = chain(s)
cm = centimetre(s)
dc = double crochet
htr = half treble
mm = millimetres
patt = pattern
rep = repeat
RS = right side
ss = slip stitch
st(s) = stitch(es)
tr = treble
WS = wrong side

MAIN PIECE:

With 4.00mm (UK 8) hook and A, make 40ch.

Foundation row: (RS) 1htr into 3rd ch from hook, 1htr into each ch to end, turn.

Patt row: 2ch (counts as first htr), miss st at base of ch, 1htr into each htr to end, working last htr into 2nd of 2ch, turn. 39 sts. Rep last row to form patt until work measures 20cm (8in) from beg, ending with a WS row and changing to B on last part of last st in A.

Edging:

With B and RS facing, 1ch (counts as first st), miss st at base of ch, 1dc into each st across top edge, 3dc into corner st, 1dc into each row end down side, 3dc into corner st, 1dc into st along other side of foundation ch, 3dc into corner st, 1dc into each row end up other side, 3dc into corner st, join with a ss into first ch. Work another round in dc, working 3dc into centre of 3dc at each corner, join with a ss into first ch. Fasten off.

TIES:

With 4.00mm (UK 8) hook and RS of work facing, join B halfway down one side edge of main piece and make 71ch.

*Next row: Ss into 2nd ch from hook, ss into each ch to end, then ss into side edge of main piece *; make 71ch and rep from * to *. Fasten off.

FLOWER MOTIFS: (make 2)

With 3.50mm (UK 9) hook and B, make a magic ring (see Note on page 21), 1ch, work 5dc into ring, change to A and join with a ss into first ch.

Next round: *1ch, (1htr, 1tr, 1htr) into next dc, 1ch, ss into same dc, rep from * 4 times more. 5 petals made. Fasten off.

taking 1.5cm (⅝in) seam allowances. Trim seam, turn RS out and press. Fold seam allowances at other short edge in, press and pin. With long seamed edge at bottom, pin this strip 5mm from lower edge and centrally between side edges of main lining piece and sew along each side and across seamed edge to form a pocket. Then sew vertical lines, every 1.5cm (⅝in) apart for smaller hooks and 2cm apart for larger hooks, through all thicknesses. Cut another strip of lining fabric 25cm wide (10in) x 14cm (5½in) high for flap. With RS facing, fold strip in half widthways and sew along each short end, taking 1.5cm (⅝in) allowances and leaving long side open. Trim seams, turn RS out and press. Fold seam allowances along long edge in, press and pin this edge in place 1.5cm (⅝in) from top edge of main lining piece. Sew along pinned edge only to form a flap to protect hooks and stop them slipping out of roll.

With WS facing, pin lining, pocket and flap piece to main crochet panel and slip stitch lining in place around all four sides.

Making up

Sew a flower motif to end of each tie.

Lining:

Cut a rectangle of fabric 27cm (10½in) wide and 23cm (9in) high for lining. Press under and machine-stitch 1.5cm (⅝in) turnings on all edges of fabric rectangle, mitring corners.

Cut a strip of lining fabric 24cm (9½in) wide x 21cm (8¼in) high for pocket. With RS facing, fold strip in half widthways and sew along one short end and long side,

Pompom slippers

Slip into a pair of soft slippers at the end of the day and put your feet up.

You can make these textured slippers with contrast-coloured edging and pompoms in a variety of sizes for men or women.

GETTING STARTED

★★ *Simple stitch pattern but concentration is required for shaping slippers.*

Size:

To fit foot size: *small[medium:large]*

Finished length: *20[23:26]cm (8[9:10¼]in)*

Note: *Figures in square brackets [ ] refer to larger sizes; where there is only one set of figures, it applies to all sizes*

How much yarn:

2 x 50g (1¾oz) balls of Wendy Emu Superwash DK in colour A – Denim (shade 1526)
1 ball in colour B – Steel Grey (shade 1508)

Hook:

4.00mm (UK 8) crochet hook

Additional items:

Piece of cardboard or pompom maker (optional)

Tension:

18 sts and 16 rows measure 10cm (4in) square over patt on 4.00mm (UK 8) hook
IT IS ESSENTIAL TO WORK TO THE STATED TENSION TO ACHIEVE SUCCESS

What you have to do:

Work toe in rounds of double crochet, increasing as directed. Continue in simple textured pattern, shaping foot by working in rows. Sew back seam, then work double crochet edging in a contrast colour. Make pompoms in contrast colour and sew to front of slippers.

The Yarn

Wendy Emu Superwash DK (approx. 119m/130 yards per 50g/1¾oz ball) contains 100% wool in a practical machine-washable format. It produces a firm fabric with good stitch definition and there is a large colour palette.

Instructions

Abbreviations:
ch = chain(s)
cm = centimetre(s)
cont = continue
dc = double crochet
patt = pattern
rep = repeat
RS = right side
ss = slip stitch
st(s) = stitch(es)
tr = treble
WS = wrong side

SLIPPERS: (make 2)
Foot:
With 4.00mm (UK 8) hook and A, make 11ch.
Foundation round: 1dc into 2nd ch from hook, 1dc into each ch to end, then cont along other side of foundation ch working 1dc into each ch, join with a ss into first dc. 20 sts.
1st round: 1ch (does not count as a st), 2dc into first st, 1dc into each of next 9 sts, 2dc into next st, 1dc into each of next 9 sts, join with a ss into first dc. 22 sts.
2nd round: 1ch, 2dc into first st, 1dc into each of next 10 sts, 2dc into next st, 1dc into each of next 10 sts, join with a ss into first dc. 24 sts.
3rd round: 1ch, 2dc into first st, 1dc into each of next 11 sts, 2dc into next st, 1dc into each of next 11 sts, join with a ss into first dc. 26 sts.
4th round: 1ch, 2dc into first st, 1dc into each of next 12 sts, 2dc into next st, 1dc into each of next 12 sts, join with a ss into first dc. 28 sts.
5th round: 1ch, 2dc into first st, 1dc into each of next 13 sts, 2dc into next st, 1dc into each of next 13 sts, join with a ss into first dc. 30 sts.
6th round: 1ch, 2dc into first st, 1dc into each of next 14 sts, 2dc into next st, 1dc into each of next 14 sts, join with a ss into first dc. 32 sts.
2nd and 3rd sizes only:
7th round: 1ch, 2dc into each of first 2 sts, 1dc into each of next 14 sts, 2dc into each of next 2 sts, 1dc into each of next 14 sts, join with a ss into first dc.
All sizes:
32[36:36] sts.
Next round: 3ch (counts as first tr), miss st at base of ch, 1dc into next st, (1tr into next st, 1dc into next st) 15[17:17]

times, join with a ss into 3rd of 3ch, turn.

1st patt round: 1ch, 1dc into same place as ss, (1tr into next dc, 1dc into next tr) 15[17:17] times, 1tr into last dc, join with a ss into first dc, turn.

2nd patt round: 3ch, (1dc into next tr, 1tr into next dc) 15[17:17] times, 1dc into last tr, join with a ss into 3rd of 3ch, turn.

Rep last 2 rounds 5[6:7] times more. Fasten off.

Shape sides and sole:

With WS facing, rejoin A in 3rd[5th:5th] st to right of last ss, 3ch, miss st at base of ch, (1dc into next tr, 1tr into next dc) 13 times, turn.

Next row: 3ch, miss first 2 sts, (1dc into next tr, 1tr into next dc) 12 times, turn.

Next row: 3ch, miss first 2 sts, (1dc into next tr, 1tr into next dc) 11 times, turn. 23 sts.

Next row: 1ch, 1dc into st at base of ch, (1tr into next dc, 1dc into next tr) 11 times, turn.

Next row: 3ch, miss st at base of ch, (1dc into next tr, 1tr into next dc) 11 times, turn.

Rep last 2 rows until sole measures 20[23:26]cm (8[9:10¼]in) from start (or until sole is required length). Fasten off.

Fold final row in half and oversew seam to form back of heel.

Edging:

With 4.00mm (UK 8) hook and RS of work facing, join B to back heel seam, 1ch, work evenly in dc around top of slipper, join with a ss into first dc. Work 1 more round in dc. Fasten off.

With B, make 2 pompoms (see Making Up instructions on page 63) and sew one to front of each slipper.

Book cover with handles

Keep your diary, sketchbook or notebook inside this distinctive cover.

Give your notebook or diary an individual look with this cover in a textured woven stitch and stripes. It has a fabric lining and can be carried around with handles that are made separately and sewn on.

GETTING STARTED

★ ★ *Attention needed as fabric is constructed in a slightly unusual way.*

Size:
To fit an A5 hardback notebook or diary

How much yarn:
1 x 50g (1¾oz) ball of Debbie Bliss Cashmerino DK in each of three colours: A – Aqua (shade 28); B – Pink (shade 27) and C – Pistachio (shade 29)

Hook:
3.50mm (UK 9) crochet hook

Additional items:
Two 25 x 14cm (10 x 5½in) rectangles of medium-weight cotton fabric
Tapestry needle
Sewing needle and thread to match yarn A

Tension:
15 sts and 19 rows measure 10cm (4in) square over pattern on 3.50mm (UK 9) hook
IT IS ESSENTIAL TO WORK TO THE STATED TENSION TO ACHIEVE SUCCESS

What you have to do:
Work cover in textured woven pattern with stripes as instructed. Work handle in two colours in the same pattern. Sew fabric lining into cover.

The Yarn
Debbie Bliss Cashmerino DK (approx. 110m/120 yards per 50g/1¾oz ball) contains 55% merino wool, 33% microfibre and 12% cashmere. It is a soft, luxurious yarn that is machine washable at a low temperature. The palette contains a lot of contemporary shades.

 Instructions

BOOK COVER:
With 3.50mm (UK 9) hook and A, make 49ch very loosely.
Foundation row: (RS) Insert hook in 2nd ch from hook, yrh and draw a loop through, insert hook in next ch, yrh and draw a loop through, yrh and draw through all 3 loops on hook, *insert hook in same ch as 2nd loop of previous st, yrh and draw a loop through, insert hook in next ch, yrh and draw a loop through, yrh and draw through all 3 loops on hook, rep from * to end, 1dc in same ch as 2nd loop of previous st, turn. 48 sts.

1st row: 1ch (does not count as st), insert hook in first st, yrh and draw through a loop, insert hook in next st, yrh and draw through a loop, yrh and draw through all 3 loops on hook, *insert hook in same st as 2nd loop

Abbreviations:
beg = beginning
ch = chain(s)
cm = centimetre(s)
dc = double crochet
rep = repeat
RS = right side
ss = slip stitch
st(s) = stitch(es)
yrh = yarn round hook

of previous st, yrh and draw through a loop, insert hook in next st, yrh and draw through a loop, yrh and draw through all 3 loops on hook, rep from * to end, 1dc in last st, remove hook from work, leaving loop on a safety-pin, do not turn.

2nd row: Starting at beg of row just worked, join in B and work 1ch, 1dc in first st, 1dc in each st to end, then remove safety-pin and pull loop of A through loop on hook, turn but do not cut off B.

3rd row: 1ch, insert hook in first st, yrh and draw through a loop, insert hook in next st, yrh and draw through a loop, yrh, draw through all 3 loops on hook, *insert hook in same st as 2nd loop of previous st, yrh and draw through a loop, insert hook in next st, yrh and draw through a loop, yrh and draw through all 3 loops on hook, rep from * to end, 1dc in last st, turn.

4th row: As 3rd row, changing to B on last st (do not cut A).

5th row: With B, as 3rd row.

6th row: As 3rd row, changing to A on last st; cut off B.

7th row: With A, as 3rd row.

8th row: As 3rd row.

9th–13th rows: 1ch, 1dc in first st, 1dc in each st to end, turn.

14th row: 1ch, insert hook in first st, yrh and draw through a loop, insert hook in next st, yrh and draw through a loop, yrh and draw through all 3 loops on hook, *insert hook in same st as 2nd loop of previous st, yrh and draw through a loop, insert hook in next st, yrh and draw through a loop, yrh and draw through all 3 loops on hook, rep from * to end, 1dc in last st, remove hook from work, leaving loop on a safety-pin, do not turn.

15th row: Using C instead of B, as 2nd row.

16th row: As 3rd row.

17th row: As 3rd row, changing to C on last st (do not cut off A).

18th row: With C, as 3rd row.

19th row: As 3rd row, changing to A on last st; cut off C.

20th row: With A, as 3rd row.

21st–26th rows: As 14th–19th rows.

27th–31st rows: 1ch, 1dc in first st, 1dc in each st to end, turn.

32nd row: As 3rd row.

33rd–39th rows: As 2nd–8th rows.

40th row: 1ch, 1dc in first st, 1dc in each st to end. Fasten off.

HANDLES:

With 3.50mm (UK 9) hook and B, make 160ch very loosely, join with a ss in first ch to form a ring.

Foundation round: 1ch (does not count as st), insert hook in first ch, yrh and draw through a loop, insert hook in next ch, yrh and draw through a loop, yrh and draw through all 3 loops on hook, * insert hook in same ch as 2nd loop of previous st, yrh and draw through a loop, insert hook in next ch, yrh and draw through a loop, yrh and draw through all 3 loops on hook, rep from * to end, join with a ss in first st.

1st round: 1ch (does not count as st), insert hook in first st, yrh and draw through a loop, insert hook in next st, yrh and draw through a loop, yrh and draw through all 3 loops on hook, * insert hook in same st as 2nd loop of previous st, yrh and draw through a loop, insert hook in next st, yrh and draw through a loop, yrh and draw through all 3 loops on hook, rep from * to end, join with a ss in first st, joining in C (do not cut off B).

2nd round: With C, as 1st round. Fasten off C.

3rd and 4th rounds: With B, as 1st round.

5th round: Ss in each st.

6th round: Carrying yarn loosely across back of work, ss in first ch of foundation ch and work 1ss in each st, join with a ss in first st. Fasten off.

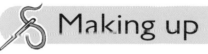

Making up

Weave in all loose ends. Finish one long edge of each cotton rectangle with a narrow double hem, then turn in 1.5cm (⅝in) on each of the remaining edges. Place each fabric lining piece RS up on inside of book cover and pin in place. Using matching sewing thread, oversew edge of book cover and folded edge of fabric together to form pockets for hard covers of book.

Slip cover on to book. Press handle and pin, then stitch it in place as shown in photographs.

Gift charms

Take your wrapping to another level with these distinctive crochet charms.

Whatever the occasion, you can give a gift package a personal touch with these cute decorative charms worked in double crochet.

GETTING STARTED

 Easy to make but these tiny items require a lot of attention to detail.

Size:

Each charm measures approximately 7–9cm (2¾–3½in) tall; test guage with the Heart and adjust hook size if necessary.

How much yarn:

1 x 25g (1oz) ball of Patons FaB DK in each of six colours: A – White (shade 02306); B – Green (shade 02329); C – Brown (shade 02309); D – Turquoise (shade 02315); E – Peach (shade 02303) and F – Red (shade 02323)

Hook:

4.00mm (UK 8) crochet hook

Additional items:

Christmas tree: Polyester toy filling; 20cm (8in) of 3mm- (⅛in-) wide green ribbon; star bead

Horseshoe: White pipe cleaner, 25cm (10in) long; 20cm (8in) of 3mm- (⅛in-) wide white ribbon; 11 x 6mm (8 x ⅛in) pearl beads

Giftbox: Polyester toy filling; 20cm (8in) of 3mm- (⅛in-) wide white ribbon; 90cm (1 yard) of coordinating sheer blue ribbon

Starfish: Polyester toy filling; 20cm (8in) of 3mm- (⅛in-) wide peach ribbon; 15 x 6mm (¼in-) pearl beads

Heart: polyester toy filling; 20cm (8in) of 3mm- (⅛in-) wide red ribbon

What you have to do:

Work each charm in double crochet. Shape and add stuffing as directed. Add decorative touches and a ribbon hanging loop to each charm as instructed.

The Yarn

Patons Fab DK (approx. 68m per 25g/1oz ball) is 100% acrylic. Good for toys, it is available in small balls and many colours.

 **Instructions**

CHRISTMAS TREE CHARM:

Tree body:

With 4.00mm (UK 8) hook and B, make a magic circle as foll: Wind B several times around tip of left forefinger. Carefully slip ring off finger, insert hook into ring, pull yarn through and make 1ch, then work 4dc in ring, join with a ss in first dc. Pull end of yarn gently to close ring. 4 sts. Marking beg of each round, work in continuous rounds with WS facing as foll: *

1st round: 1dc in each st to end.

2nd round: 2dc in each st to end. 8 sts.

3rd round: (2dc in next st, 1dc in next st) to end. 12 sts.

4th round: As 1st.

5th round: (2dc in next st, 1dc in each of next 2 sts) to end. 16 sts.

6th round: As 1st.

7th round: (2dc in next st, 1dc in each of next 3 sts) to end. 20 sts.

8th round: As 1st.

9th round: (Working in front loops only, dc2tog over next 2 sts) to end. 10 sts.

10th and 11th rounds: As 1st and 2nd. 20 sts.

12th round: (2dc in next st, 1dc in each of next 4 sts) to end. 24 sts.

13th round: As 1st.

14th round: (2dc in next st, 1dc in each of next 5 sts) to end. 28 sts.

15th round: As 1st.

Abbreviations:
beg = beginning
ch = chain(s)
cm = centimetre(s)
cont = continue
dc = double crochet
dc2tog = (insert hook in next st, yrh and draw a loop through) twice, yrh and draw through all 3 loops
dec = decreased
foll = follows
rem = remains
rep = repeat
RS = right side
ss = slip stitch
st(s) = stitch(es)
WS = wrong side
yrh = yarn round hook

16th round: (2dc in next st, 1dc in each of next 6 sts) to end. 32 sts.
17th round: As 9th. 16 sts.
18th round: As 9th, but working in both loops. 8 sts. Stuff shape firmly, then work (dc2tog over next 2 sts) until gap is closed. Fasten off.

Tree trunk:
With 4.00mm (UK 8) hook and C, make a magic circle (see page 97) and make 1ch, then work 6dc in ring, join with a ss in first dc. 6 sts.
1st–3rd rounds: 1dc in each st to end. Fasten off, leaving a 30cm (12in) tail for sewing trunk to tree body.

Garlands:
With 4.00mm (UK 8) hook and A, make 25ch. Fasten off, leaving a 30cm (12in) tail for sewing to upper tree tier.
Make another 40ch garland for sewing to lower tree tier.

HORSESHOE CHARM:
With 4.00mm (UK 8) hook and A, work as Christmas tree charm to *.
1st and 2nd rounds: 1dc in each st to end. 4 sts.
3rd round: 2dc in first st, 1dc in each of next 3 sts. 5 sts.
4th round: 1dc in each st to end.

5th round: 2dc in first st, 1dc in each of next 4 sts. 6 sts.
6th–37th rounds: 1dc in each st to end.
38th round: Dc2tog over first 2 sts, 1dc in each of next 4 sts. 5 sts.
39th round: 1dc in each st to end.
40th round: Dc2tog over first 2 sts, 1dc in each of next 3 sts. 4 sts. Carefully insert pipe cleaner into centre of tube and work rest of sts around end of pipe cleaner.
41st and 42nd rounds: 1dc in each st to end. Trim off excess pipe cleaner.
43rd round: (Dc2tog) twice.
Fasten off.

GIFTBOX CHARM:
Top and base: (make 2)
With 4.00mm (UK 8) hook and D, make 8ch.
Foundation row: (RS) 1dc in 2nd ch from hook, 1dc in each ch to end, turn. 7 sts.
1st–6th rows: 1ch (counts as first dc), miss st at base of ch, 1dc in each st to end, turn. Fasten off.
Side panel:
With 4.00mm (UK 8) hook and D, make 14ch. Work foundation row as Top and base. 13 sts. Cont in rows of dc, working in stripes of 2 rows each D and A (always changing to new colour on last part of last st in old colour), until 28 rows in all have been completed.
Last row: Fold work in half with RS facing so foundation edge lines up with row just worked, now work to end in dc through adjacent pairs of sts to form an open tube. Fasten off. Turn tube RS out.

STARFISH CHARM: (make 2 but do not fasten off at end of second piece)
Worked with RS facing.
With 4.00mm (UK 8) hook and E, work as Christmas tree charm to *, working 5dc instead of 4dc in ring.
1st round: 2dc in each st to end. 10 sts.
2nd round: (2dc in next st, 1dc in next st) to end. 15 sts.

3rd round: (2dc in next st, 1dc in each of next 2 sts) to end. 20 sts.

4th round: (1dc in next st, 6ch, miss 1ch, 1dc in each of next 5ch, ss in each of next 3 sts) 5 times.

5th round: 1dc in each st all round. Fasten off.

HEART CHARM: (make 2 hearts in same way)
First heart top curve:
With 4.00mm (UK 8) hook and F, make a magic circle as Christmas tree charm, 1ch, work 4dc in ring, turn.

1st row: 1ch (does not count as a st), (1dc in next st, 2dc in next st) twice, turn. 6 sts.

2nd row: 1ch, (1dc in each of next 2 sts, 2dc in next st) twice. 8 sts. Fasten off.

Second heart top curve:
Make a second heart top curve in same way but do not fasten off at end.

Join curves:
Next row: 1ch, work 5dc along straight edge of heart curve, then 5dc along straight edge of other heart curve, turn. 10 sts.

Next row: 1ch, 1dc in each st, turn.

Next row: 1ch, 1dc in each st to last st, turn. 1 st dec. Rep last row until 1 st rem. Fasten off.

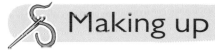

Making up

CHRISTMAS TREE CHARM:
Stuff trunk and sew to middle of tree body base. Sew garlands in place in loops of 5ch to each tree tier. Sew star bead to top of tree. Thread ribbon through top of tree, below star, and tie in a knot to make a hanging loop.

HORSESHOE CHARM:
Bend horseshoe into a U-shape. Spacing evenly, sew beads on to one side of horseshoe. Thread ribbon through centre of top of horseshoe and tie in a knot to make a hanging loop.

GIFTBOX CHARM:
Slip stitch base to one end of tube. Stuff well with toy filling, then slip stitch top in position. Tie coordinating ribbon around giftbox and tie in a bow on top of box. Thread white ribbon through centre of top of charm and tie in a knot to make a hanging loop.

STARFISH CHARM:
With WS facing, place one starfish on top of the other, now work in dc through adjacent pairs of sts around outer edge to join, leaving a gap at end to insert filling. Stuff firmly through gap and then cont in dc to close gap. Fasten off. Sew one pearl bead to tip of each 'arm' and another two beads along arm. Thread ribbon through top of one arm and tie in a knot to make a hanging loop.

HEART CHARM:
With WS facing, slip stitch hearts together around outer edge, leaving a small gap for stuffing. Insert stuffing and then close gap. Thread ribbon through centre of curves at top of heart and tie in a knot to make a hanging loop.

Laptop case

Protect your computer with this bright funky cover.

Worked in easy double crochet and a bright, funky yarn, this zipped computer case has protective padding within its sewn lining.

The Yarn
King Cole Wicked DK (approx. 290m/316 yards per 100g/3½oz ball) contains 100% premium acrylic. This easy-care yarn has coloured threads bound onto its plain background colour; great for interesting patterns.

GETTING STARTED

⭐ *Easy fabric without shaping but a good result requires neat sewing and finishing.*

Size:
Finished case measures approximately 39cm (15½in) wide x 27cm (10½in) high

How much yarn:
2 x 100g (3½oz) balls of King Cole Wicked DK in Black (shade 720)

Hook:
4.00mm (UK 8) crochet hook

Additional items:
Pink zip fastener, 56cm (22in) long;
Two pieces of felt, each 37 x 25cm (14½ x 10in)
60cm (⅝in) of pink lining fabric 90cm- (36 yard-) wide

Matching sewing thread and needle

Tension:
16.5 sts and 22 rows measure 10cm (4in) square over dc on 4.00mm (UK 8) hook
IT IS ESSENTIAL TO WORK TO THE STATED TENSION TO ACHIEVE SUCCESS

What you have to do:
Work each side of case in double crochet, adding a double crochet edging all around. Add a double crochet zip edging across top and part-way down sides. Crochet back and front of case together on right side of work. Sew in zip fastener. Add padding and sewn fabric lining.

Instructions

Abbreviations:

beg = beginning
ch = chain(s)
cm = centimetre(s)
dc = double crochet
rep = repeat
RS = right side
ss = slip stitch
st(s) = stitch(es)
tog = together
WS = wrong side

FRONT:

With 4.00mm (UK 8) hook make 62ch.

Foundation row: (RS) 1dc into 2nd ch from hook, 1dc into each ch to end, turn. 61dc.

1st row: 1ch (does not count as a st), 1dc into each dc to end, turn. Rep last row until work measures 25cm (10in) from beg, ending with a WS row. Turn at end of final row but do not fasten off.

Edging:

With 4.00mm (UK 8) hook and RS of Front facing, 1ch (does not count as a st), 1dc into each dc across top edge, 2dc into corner st, 1dc into each row end down side, 2dc into corner st, 1dc into each ch of other side of foundation ch, 2dc into corner st and 1dc into each row end up

other side, 1 dc into same place as first dc, join with a ss into first dc. Fasten off.

Zip edging:

With 4.00mm (UK 8) hook and RS of Front facing, join yarn to right-hand side 8cm (3in) down from top corner, 1ch (does not count as a st), 1dc into each dc up side, 2dc into corner st, 1dc into each dc across top edge, 2dc into corner st, 1dc into each dc down left side for 8cm (3in). Fasten off.

BACK:

Work as given for Front, but do not fasten off at end of zip edging.

Joining Back and Front:

Place Back and Front with WS tog and zip edging across top. With 4.00mm (UK 8) hook, RS facing and using yarn attached, crochet pieces tog down first side, across lower edge and up second side to zip edging by working 1dc through dc on both edges simultaneously and 2dc into each corner dc. Fasten off.

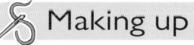 # Making up

Use finished case as a template to cut out two rectangles of pink lining fabric to same size as case. Sew in zip fastener down sides and across top of case between zip edgings.

Lining:

Place one piece of felt centrally on WS of each side of case and lightly slip stitch edges in place so that sts do not show through on RS. Turn under and press a 1cm (⅜in) hem along one long edge of each piece of lining fabric for top. With RS facing, beg and end at point 8cm (3in) below fold, pin then tack, side and lower edges. Slip lining inside crochet case to check size and adjust if necessary. Sew seam. Snip into corners. With WS facing, sew neatly to zip tape.

Pastel patchwork bag

A really pretty variegated yarn is used for the patchwork squares in this lovely bag.

This practical square bag with a base and gussets is constructed from pretty patchwork motifs – all with the same variegated pastel shades in the centre surrounded by a toning plain colour.

GETTING STARTED

★★ *Motifs are simple to make but neat sewing is required to ensure a good finished result.*

Size:
Bag is 33cm (13in) wide x 34cm (13½in) high x 11cm (4¼in) deep, excluding handles

How much yarn:
2 x 100g (3½oz) skeins of Manos del Uruguay Fair Trade Wool Clasica in each of colour A – Athena (shade 8931) and colour B – Mississippi (shade 2370)

Hook:
5.00mm (UK 6) crochet hook

Additional items:
60cm (1¾ yards) of 90cm- (36in-) wide quilted fabric (see Note on page 106)
Sewing needle and matching thread

Tension:
Each finished square measures 11cm (4¼in) on 5.00mm (UK 6) hook
IT IS ESSENTIAL TO WORK TO THE STATED TENSION TO ACHIEVE SUCCESS

What you have to do:
Make square motifs in two colours – one variegated and one plain. Sew squares together to form bag. Make handles in rows of double crochet. Sew quilted lining for bag.

The Yarn
Manos del Uruguay Fair Trade Wool Clasica (approx. 126m/137 yards per 100g/3½oz ball) is a blend of Corriedale and Merino wool. It is handwash only.

Instructions

Abbreviations:

ch = chain
cm = centimetre(s)
cont = continue
dc = double crochet
foll = follows
RS = right side
sp = space
ss = slip stitch
tr = treble
WS = wrong side

Note: If you can buy ready-quilted fabric, with a layer of wadding between two outer layers of fabric, choose one that is not too bulky. To make your own, sandwich layers of fabric and wadding and machine-stitch diagonal lines of stitching to form a diamond-patterned grid of quilting stitches.

SQUARE MOTIF: (make 27)
With 5.00mm (UK 6) hook and A, make 5ch, join with a ss into first ch to form a ring.

1st round: 5ch, (3tr into ring, 2ch) 3 times, 2tr into ring, join with a ss into 3rd of 5ch.

2nd round: Ss into next ch sp, 7ch, (2tr into sp, 1tr into each of next 3tr, 2tr into next sp, 4ch) 3 times, 2tr into sp, 1tr into each of next 3tr, 1tr into next sp, join with a ss into 3rd of 7ch, changing to B.

3rd round: With B, ss into next ch sp, (5dc into ch sp, 1dc into each of next 7tr) 4 times, join with a ss into first dc.

4th round: 1dc into each of first 2dc, (3dc into next dc, 1dc into each of next

1dc) 3 times, 3dc into next dc, 1dc into each of last 9dc, join with a ss into first dc. Fasten off.

BAG:

Darn in ends, then press squares under a slightly damp cloth with a warm iron. Sew squares together to make nine rows with three squares in each, then join seven rows together to form bag front, base and back. Sew in two remaining rows to form side gussets.

Border:

With 5.00mm (UK 6) hook and RS facing, join B to one side seam at top edge and cont as foll:

1st round: 1ch (does not count as a st), 1dc into each dc along squares and 1dc in each seam-end between squares, join with a ss in first dc. 128dc.

2nd round: 1ch, working into back loop only of each st, work 1dc into each dc to end, join with a ss into first dc.

3rd and 4th rounds: Work in dc, inserting hook into both loops of each st as usual. Fasten off.

HANDLE: (make 2)

With 5.00mm (UK 6) hook and B, leave a tail of at least 20cm (8in), then make 59ch.

Foundation row: 1dc into 2nd ch from hook, 1dc into each ch to end, turn. 58 sts.

1st-3rd rows: 1ch (does not count as a st), 1dc into each dc to end, turn.

4th row: 1ch, working into back loop only of each st,

1dc into each dc to end, turn.

5th–7th rows: As 1st-3rd rows. Fold handle in half, along top of 3rd row and join each st of 7th row to corresponding ch at opposite edge with a row of ss. Fasten off, leaving a long tail.

Making up

Fold top border to inside and pin in place. Flatten bag and cut a rectangle of lining fabric to fit bag, allowing 1.5cm (⅝in) extra all round. With wrong sides of fabric together, sew side seams 6mm (¼in) in from edges, then turn so that right sides are together and stitch side seams again, 9mm (⅜in) from folded edges and trapping raw edges inside. Flatten corners and fold upwards against side seam, then stitch across corners to form gusset. Trim off excess fabric at corners. Place lining inside bag, matching side seams and tucking raw edge under fold of bag border. Pin in place, then slip stitch edge of bag border to lining. Using picture as a guide to positioning, sew on handles to inside of border, stitching neatly through inner border, lining and outer border.

Long gloves with a bow

Wear these long gloves pulled up or ruched down to suit your outfit. Either way they'll keep your fingers warm.

Worked in rounds of simple stitches with a rib effect at the cuff, these gloves feature a decorative band of surface crochet with ties at the wrist.

GETTING STARTED

★★★ *These gloves use simple stitches but you will need to be accurate on the stitch count when working fingers and thumb.*

Size:
Around palm; 20cm (8in)
Length: 40cm (16in)

How much yarn:
3 x 50g (1¾oz) balls of King Cole Merino Blend 4-Ply in colour A – Grey (shade 36)
1 ball in colour B – Pink (shade 787)

Hooks:
3.00mm (UK 11) crochet hook
2.00mm (UK 14) crochet hook

Tension:
25 sts and 18 rows measure 10cm (4in) over patt on 3.00mm (UK 11) hook
IT IS ESSENTIAL TO WORK TO THE STATED TENSION TO ACHIEVE SUCCESS

What you have to do:
Work in alternate rounds of double crochet and trebles. Add coloured bands of surface crochet at wrist finished with short double crochet ties. Shape for thumb and fingers as directed. Work a single row of crochet rib at top edge.

The Yarn
King Cole Merino Blend 4-Ply (approx. 180m/ 196 yards per 50g/1¾oz ball) contains 100% pure new wool in a machine-washable format. It is available in a wide range of colours and produces a soft, yet practical, fabric.

 Instructions

RIGHT GLOVE:
With 3.00mm (UK 11) hook and A, make 58ch, join with a ss in first ch to form a ring taking care not to twist ch.
Foundation round: 1ch (does not count as a st), 1dc in same ch as ss, 1dc in each ch to end, join with a ss in first dc, turn. 58 sts.
1st patt round: (RS) 3ch (counts as first tr), miss st at base of ch, 1tr in each st to end, join with a ss in 3rd of 3ch, turn. Always work with RS outside – dc rounds are worked around inside (WS) of glove.

2nd patt round: 1ch, 1dc in same place as ss, 1dc in each st to end, join with a ss in first dc, turn.
These 2 rounds form patt. Patt 6 more rounds.
1st dec round: 3ch, miss st at base of ch, 1tr in each of next 4 sts, tr2tog, 1tr in each of next 15 sts, tr2tog, 1tr in each of next 10 sts, tr2tog, 1tr in each of next 15 sts, tr2tog, 1tr in each of last 5 sts, join with a ss in top of 3ch, turn. 54 sts.
Patt 9 rounds.
2nd dec round: 3ch, miss st at base of ch, 1tr in each of

Abbreviations:
beg = beginning
ch = chain
cm = centimetre(s)
cont = continue
dc = double crochet
dc2tog = (insert hook in next st, yrh and draw loop through) twice, yrh and draw through all 3 loops
dec = decrease
foll = following
inc = increase(d)(s)
patt = pattern
rem = remaining
rep = repeat
RS = right side
sp = space
ss = slip stitch
st(s) = stitch(es)
tr = treble
tr2(3)tog = (yrh, insert hook in next st, yrh and draw loop through, yrh and draw through first 2 loops) 2(3) times, yrh and draw through all 3(4) loops
WS = wrong side
yrh = yarn round hook

next 3 sts, tr2tog, 1tr in each of next 15 sts, tr2tog, 1tr in each of next 8 sts, tr2tog, 1tr in each of next 15 sts, tr2tog, 1tr in each of last 4 sts, join with a ss in top of 3ch, turn. 50 sts.
Patt 13 rounds, ending with a 2nd patt round.

Wristband:
1st wrist round: As 1st patt round.
2nd wrist round: As 1st patt round but work around inside (WS) of glove.
3rd wrist round: As 1st patt round.
4th wrist round: As 2nd patt round.
Slip working loop on a safety pin to prevent it unravelling. Do not fasten off A.
Surface crochet: Holding yarn on WS (inside of work), attach B to 3ch at beg of 1st wrist round, insert hook in sp between last tr of round and 3ch at beg, yrh and draw loop through, *insert hook in sp between 3ch and next tr, yrh and pull loop through and through loop on hook, rep from

* into each sp between sts to end, then work another round into the same round of the wristband at the left of the first. At the end of the second round, insert hook, yrh and pull loop through. Cut yarn leaving 100cm (40in) end for tie.
Ties: Insert hook through join of surface crochet, yrh and draw loop through, (10ch, 1dc in 2nd ch from hook, 1dc in each ch, 1ss in join of surface crochet) twice. Fasten off. Work 2 rounds of surface crochet around 2nd wrist round but do not work ties.
Work 2 rounds of surface crochet around 3rd wrist round working ties as given. **

Shape thumb:
Place working loop back on hook and cont in A.
1st inc round: (RS) 3ch, miss st at base of ch, 1tr in each of next 26 sts, 2tr in next st, 1tr in each of next 2 sts, 2tr in next st, 1tr in each of rem 19 sts, join with a ss in top of 3ch, turn. 2 sts inc.
Patt 1 round.
2nd inc round: 3ch, miss st at base of ch, 1tr in each of next 26 sts, 2tr in next st, 1tr in each of next 4 sts, 2tr in next st, 1tr in each of rem 19 sts, join with a ss in top of 3ch, turn. 2 sts inc. Patt 1 round.
3rd inc round: 3ch, miss st at base of ch, 1tr in each of next 26 sts, 2tr in next st, 1tr in each of next 6 sts, 2tr in next st, 1tr in each of rem 19 sts, join with ss in top of 3ch, turn. 2 sts inc.
Patt 1 round.
Cont to inc in this way on next 4 RS rounds, working 2 extra sts between incs on each round. 64 sts.
Next round: (WS) 1ch, 1dc in same place as ss, 1dc in each of next 20 sts, 2ch,

miss next 16 sts for thumb opening, 1dc in each of rem 27 sts, join with a ss in first dc, turn.

***Next round:** 3ch, miss st at base of ch, 1tr in each dc and each of the 2ch at thumb opening, join with a ss in top of 3ch, turn. 50 sts.
Patt 6 rounds.

Little finger:
1st round: (WS) 1ch, 1dc in same place as ss, 1dc in each of next 4 sts, 3ch, miss 40 sts, 1dc in each of last 5 sts, join with a ss in first dc, turn.
2nd round: 3ch, miss st at base of ch, 1tr in each of next 5 sts, 1tr in each of 3ch, 1tr in each of next 4 sts, join with a ss in top of 3ch, turn. 13 sts.
Patt 7 rounds.
Last round: 3ch, miss st at base of ch, (tr3tog) 4 times, join with a ss in top of 3ch. 5 sts. Fasten off.

Ring finger:
1st round: With WS facing, rejoin A to first of 3ch at base of little finger, 1ch, 1dc in same place as join, dc2tog over next 2ch, 1dc in each of next 6 sts, 3ch, miss 28 sts, 1dc in each of next 6 sts, join with a ss in first dc, turn.
2nd round: 3ch, miss st at base of ch, 1tr in each of next 6 sts, 1tr in next ch, tr2tog over next 2ch, 1tr in each of next 7 sts, join with a ss in top of 3ch, turn. 16 sts.
Patt 9 rounds.
Last round: 3ch, miss st at base of ch, (tr3tog) 5 times, join with a ss in top of 3ch. 6 sts. Fasten off.

Middle finger:
1st round: With WS facing, rejoin A to first of 3ch at base of ring finger, 1ch, 1dc in same place as join, dc2tog over next 2ch, 1dc in each of next 7 sts, 3ch, miss 14 sts, 1dc in each of next 7 sts, join with a ss in first dc, turn.
2nd round: 3ch, miss st at base of ch, 1tr in each of next 7 sts, 1tr in next ch, tr2tog over next 2ch, 1tr in each of next 8 sts, join with a ss in top of 3ch, turn. 18 sts.
Patt 11 rounds.
Last round: 3ch, miss st at base of ch, tr2tog, (tr3tog) 5 times, join with a ss in top of 3ch. 7 sts. Fasten off.

Index finger:
1st round: With WS facing, rejoin A to first of 3ch at base of middle finger, 1ch, 1dc in same place as join, dc2tog over next 2ch, 1dc in each of next 14 sts, join with a ss in first dc, turn. 16 sts.
Patt 10 rounds.
Last round: 3ch, miss st at base of ch, (tr3tog) 5 times, join with a ss in top of 3ch. 6 sts. Fasten off.

Thumb:
With WS facing, rejoin A to first of 2ch of thumb opening, 1ch, 1dc in same place as join, 1dc in next ch, 1dc in each of 16 sts, join with a ss in first dc, turn. 18 sts.
Patt 8 rounds.
Last round: 3ch, miss st at base of ch, tr2tog, (tr3tog) 5 times, join with a ss in top of 3ch. 7 sts. Fasten off.

Top rib:
With 2.00mm (UK 14) hook and RS facing, join A around 3ch at beg of 1st patt round at top edge, working over the foundation round work, 3ch, (inserting hook from front and from right to left, work 1tr around stem of next tr, inserting hook from back and from right to left, work 1tr around stem of foll tr) to last st, inserting hook from front and from right to left, work 1tr around stem of next tr, join with a ss in top of 3ch. Fasten off.

LEFT GLOVE:
Work as given for Right glove to **.

Shape thumb:
Place working loop of A back on hook.
1st inc round: (RS) 3ch, miss st at base of ch, 1tr in each of next 18 sts, 2tr in next st, 1tr in each of next 2 sts, 2tr in next st, 1tr in each of rem 27 sts, join with a ss in top of 3ch, turn. 2 sts inc.
Patt 1 round.
2nd inc round: 3ch, miss st at base of ch, 1tr in each of next 18 sts, 2tr in next st, 1tr in each of next 4 sts, 2tr in next st, 1tr in each of rem 27 sts, join with a ss in top of 3ch, turn. 2 sts inc.
Patt 1 round.
3rd inc round: 3ch, miss st at base of ch, 1tr in each of next 18 sts, 2tr in next st, 1tr in each of next 6 sts, 2tr in next st, 1tr in each of rem 27 sts, join with ss in top of 3ch, turn. 2 sts inc.
Patt 1 round.
Cont to inc in this way on next 4 RS rounds, working 2 extra sts between incs on each round. 64 sts.
Next round: (WS) 1ch, 1dc in same place as ss, 1dc in each of next 28 sts, 2ch, miss next 16 sts for thumb opening, 1dc in each of rem 19 sts, join with a ss in first dc, turn.
Complete as given for Right glove from ***.

✂ Making up

Darn in all ends. Press lightly. Make a single knot in each pair of ties.

Oversized chevron beanie

Follow the trend for slouchy headwear with this amazing hat.

This big, baggy beanie has a rib-effect headband and an attractive chevron pattern in colourful stripes. The multi-colour pompom adds the finishing touch.

GETTING STARTED

★★ *Pattern is simple to follow once the chevrons appear.*

Size:
To fit an average-sized woman's head with circumference of approximately 56cm (22in)

How much yarn:
2 x 50g (1¾oz) balls of King Cole Merino Blend DK in colour A – Graphite (shade 702)
1 ball in each of 3 other colours: B – Oatmeal (shade 41); C – Scarlet (shade 9) and D – Olive (shade 69)

Hooks:
3.50mm (UK 9) crochet hook
4.00mm (UK 8) crochet hook

Additional items:
Sewing needle and matching thread
Piece of cardboard or pompom maker (optional)

Tension:
12 sts (1 patt) measure 7cm (2¾in) over chevron patt on 4.00mm (UK 8) hook
IT IS ESSENTIAL TO WORK TO THE STATED TENSION TO ACHIEVE SUCCESS

What you have to do:
Work headband first in one colour and rows of half trebles worked into front or back loop only of stitches to resemble ribbing. Pick up stitches for main part of hat from one long edge of headband. Work main pattern in trebles and stripes of chevron pattern, shaping as directed. Make pompom and sew to top of hat.

The Yarn
King Cole Merino Blend DK (approx. 112m/122 yards per 50g/1¾oz ball) is 100% pure wool in a practical superwash format. It makes an attractive fabric and there is a wide colour range.

Instructions

Abbreviations:

alt = alternate
ch = chain(s)
cm = centimetre(s)
dc = double crochet
dec = decrease
foll = follow(s)(ing)
htr = half treble
patt = pattern
rep = repeat
RS = right side
sp = space
st(s) = stitch(es)
tr = treble
tr2(4)tog = work 1tr into next 2(4) sts as directed leaving last loop of each on hook, yrh and draw through all 3(5) loops on hook
yrh = yarn round hook

Note:

When working main part of Hat, always join in new colour on last part of last st in old colour. Work over tail of old colour for about 5cm (2in) to enclose it, but leave a 15cm (6in) tail of new colour to use when joining seam.

HAT:
Headband:

With 3.50mm (UK 9) hook and A, make 16ch.

Foundation row: (RS) 1htr into 3rd ch from hook, 1htr into each ch to end, turn. 15 sts.

1st row: 2ch (counts as first htr), miss st at base of ch, 1htr into front loop only of each htr to end, working last htr in 2nd of 2ch, turn.

2nd row: 2ch, miss st at base of ch, 1htr into back loop only of each htr to end, working last htr in 2nd of 2ch, turn.

Rep last 2 rows 34 more times, then work 1st row again. 72 rows in all. Fasten off. With 4.00mm (UK 8) hook and RS of Headband facing, join B at right-hand end of one long edge.

1st row: 1ch (counts as first dc), 1dc into side edge of each row to end, turn. 73 sts.

2nd row: 3ch (counts as first tr), 1tr into st at base of ch, *1tr into each of next 7dc, (1tr, 1ch, 1tr) into next dc, rep from * to last 8 sts, 1tr into each of next 7dc, 2tr into 1ch, turn. 91 sts.

3rd row: 3ch, 1tr into st at base of ch, *1tr into each of next 9tr, (1tr, 1ch, 1tr)

into 1ch sp, rep from * to last 10 sts, 1tr into each of next 9tr; 2tr into 3rd of 3ch, turn. 109 sts. Fasten off B and join in C.

Patt row: 3ch, 1tr into first tr, *1tr into each of next 4tr; tr2tog over (next and foll alt tr), 1tr into each of next 4tr, (1tr, 1ch, 1tr) into 1ch sp, rep from * to last 12 sts, 1tr into each of next 4tr; tr2tog as set, 1tr into each of next 4tr, 2tr into 3rd of 3ch, turn. Fasten off C. Rep patt row throughout in colour sequence as foll: 2 rows A, 1 row D, 1 row B, 2 rows C, 1 row A, 1 row D, 2 rows B, 1 row C, 1 row A and 1 row D. Do not fasten off D.

Shape top:

1st dec row: With D, 3ch, miss st at base of ch, *1tr into each of next 4tr, tr2tog as set, 1tr into each of next 4tr, miss 1ch sp, rep from * to last 12 sts, 1tr into each of next 4tr, tr2tog as set, 1tr into each of next 4tr, 1tr into 3rd of 3ch, turn. 83 sts
Fasten off D and join in B.

2nd dec row: 3ch, miss st at base of ch, *1tr into each of next 3tr, tr2tog as set, 1tr into each of next 3tr, rep from * to last st, 1tr into 3rd of 3ch, turn. 65 sts.
Fasten off B and join in C.

3rd dec row: 3ch, miss st at base of ch, *1tr into next tr, tr4tog over (1st, 2nd, 4th and 5th foll tr), 1tr into next tr, rep from * to last st, 1tr into 3rd of 3ch. 29 sts. Fasten off leaving a long tail.

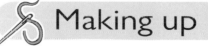

Making up

Starting at lower edge, join back seam using yarn tails to match each stripe. Thread final yarn tail into needle and run in and out along top edge, gather up tightly and backstitch securely closed. Using all four colours, make a pompom about 7cm (2¾in) in diameter (see Making Up instructions on page 63) and sew to gathered top of hat.

Zig-zag scarf

A simple stitch worked in increases and decreases gives
the chevron-shape to this scarf.

This chevron pattern scarf, worked in trebles and graduated shades of one colour, makes a striking accessory to liven up your wardrobe.

GETTING STARTED

★ *Easy pattern to follow once the foundation row has been established.*

Size:

Scarf measures 13cm (5in) wide x 132cm (52in) long, excluding fringing

How much yarn:

1 x 50g (1¾oz) ball of Debbie Bliss Baby Cashmerino in each of four colours: A – Peppermint Green (shade 003); B – Pale Green (shade 002); C – Aqua Green (shade 040) and D – Dark Turquoise (shade 203)

Hook:

4.00mm (UK 8) crochet hook

Tension:

10 sts (1 patt rep) measure 6cm and 4 rows (1 patt rep) measure 4cm (1½in) on 4.00mm (UK 8) hook IT IS ESSENTIAL TO WORK TO THE STATED TENSION TO ACHIEVE SUCCESS

What you have to do:

Make long length of foundation chain. Work throughout in trebles, creating chevron pattern by mass increasing and decreasing stitches at intervals throughout each row. Work each row in a different colour. Knot matching-coloured tassels into row ends.

The Yarn

Debbie Bliss Cashmerino DK (approx. 110m/120 yards per 50g/1¾oz ball) contains 55% merino wool, 33% microfibre and 12% cashmere. It is extremely soft, can be machine washed and there is a wide palette of beautiful colours to choose from.

Instructions

Abbreviations:

ch = chain(s)

cm = centimetre(s)

patt = pattern

rep = repeat

RS = right side

st(s) = stitch(es)

tr = treble(s)

tr3tog = work 1tr
in each of next 3 sts
leaving last loop of each
on hook, yarn round
hook and draw through
all 4 loops

SCARF:

With 4.00mm (UK 8) hook and A, make 224ch loosely.

Foundation row: (RS) With A, 1tr into 4th ch from hook, *1tr into each of next 3ch, over next 3ch work tr3tog, 1tr into each of next 3ch, 3tr into next ch, rep from * ending last rep with 2tr into last ch and joining in B for final part of last st, turn. 221 sts.

Patt row: With B, 3ch (counts as first tr), 1tr into first st at base of 3ch, *1tr into each of next 3tr, over next 3 sts work tr3tog, 1tr into each of next 3tr, 3tr into next tr, rep from * ending last rep with 2tr into top of 3ch and joining in C for final part of last st, turn.

Rep last row throughout to form patt, working in stripe sequence of 1 row C, 1 row D, (1 row each A, B, C and D) twice, then 1 row A (13 rows in all). Fasten off.

Tassels:

Cut 5 x 30cm (12in) lengths of yarn for each tassel. Knot a tassel into each row end across short ends of Scarf, matching stripe and tassel colours. Trim tassels evenly.

HOW TO
WORK THE PATTERN

The pattern is formed by increasing and decreasing stitches at regular intervals through the row.

1 Make a foundation chain of 224 chains. To work the foundation row, begin with one treble into the fourth chain from the hook. Begin the repeat sequence by working one treble into each of the next three chains.

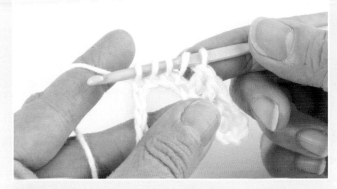

2 Now work three trebles together into the next three chains. To do this, work one treble into each of the three chains leaving the last loop of each on the hook, then take the yarn round the hook and draw it through all four loops.

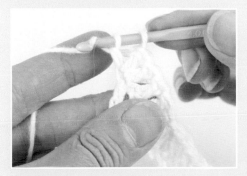

3 Work one treble into each of the next three chains and then three trebles into the next chain to complete the sequence. Repeat this sequence, ending the last repeat with two trebles into the last chain and then joining in the new colour for the last part of the stitch. Turn the work.

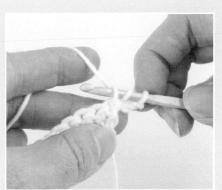

4 Make three turning chains (this counts as first treble) and work one treble into the first stitch at the base of the turning chain.

5 Begin the repeat sequence with one treble into each of the next three stitches. Over the next three stitches work three trebles together, one treble into each of the next three trebles and three trebles into the next stitch.

6 Repeat this sequence ending the last repeat with two trebles into the top of the turning chain and joining in the next colour for the final part of the last stitch. Turn the work.

7 Repeat the last row throughout to form the pattern, changing colours as instructed.

Star pin cushion

Practise your colourwork with this mini project.

Styled as an envelope with a back button fastening and worked in double crochet, this neat pincushion has a bold intarsia star motif on the front.

GETTING STARTED

⭐ ⭐ *Working colour designs by the intarsia method requires a lot of practice but this is a small design with little shaping.*

Size:
Approximately 10cm (4in) square

How much yarn:
1 x 50g (1¾oz) ball of Anchor Style Creativa Fino in each of two colours: A – White (shade 01331) and B – Red (shade 01333)

Hook:
2.50mm (UK 12) crochet hook

Additional items:
5 bobbins
1 red button
2 x 11cm (4¼in) squares of white lining fabric
Red and white sewing thread and needle
Polyester toy filling

Tension:
26 sts and 30 rows measure 10cm (4in) square over dc on 2.50mm (UK 12) hook
IT IS ESSENTIAL TO WORK TO THE STATED TENSION TO ACHIEVE SUCCESS

What you have to do:
Work in double crochet throughout. Work star motif on front using intarsia technique and working with small, separate lengths of yarn. Sew polyester-filled fabric pad for inside pincushion.

The Yarn
Anchor Style Creativa Fino (approx. 125m/ 136 yards per 50g/1¾oz ball) is 100% pure cotton in a 4-ply weight. It produces a soft fabric with a silky sheen that makes it ideal for craft projects. There is a wide range of colours.

Instructions

Abbreviations:
ch = chain(s)
cm = centimetre(s)
cont = continue
dc = double crochet
dc2tog = (insert hook in next st, yrh and draw a loop through) twice, yrh and draw through all 3 loops on hook
dec = decreased
foll = follows
patt = pattern
rem = remain
rep = repeat
RS = right side
ss = slip stitch
st(s) = stitch(es)
WS = wrong side
yrh = yarn round hook

Notes:
• Before you begin, cut three x 3m- (3-yard) lengths of A and wind on to individual bobbins. Also cut two x 2m- (2-yard) lengths of B and wind on to individual bobbins.
• When changing colour, complete last part of last stitch in old colour with new colour. To work out which bobbin to use, pick up yarn nearest to stitch being worked.
• When working in intarsia patt, do not carry yarns across back of work. Instead use individual bobbins as stated for each area of colour, twisting yarns together on WS of work when changing colour to avoid a hole forming.

FRONT:
With 2.50mm (UK 12) hook and A, make 26ch.
Foundation row: (WS) 1dc in 2nd ch from hook, 1dc in each ch to end, turn. 26 sts.
1st and 2nd rows: 1ch (counts as first dc), miss first st, 1dc in each dc to end, working last dc in turning ch, turn.
Cont in dc as set, working intarsia patt as foll:
3rd row: (RS) 4 A, join on bobbin in B, 2 B, join on bobbin in A, 14 A, join on bobbin in B, 2 B, join on bobbin in A, 4 A, turn.
4th row: 4 A, 3 B, 12 A, 2 B, 5 A, turn.
5th row: 5 A, 3 B, 10 A, 3 B, 5 A, turn.
6th row: 6 A, 3 B, 8 A, 3 B, 6 A, turn.
7th row: 6 A, 4 B, 6 A, 4 B, 6 A, turn.

8th row: 6 A, 4 B, 5 A, 4 B, 7 A, turn.
9th row: 7 A, 4 B, 4 A, 4 B, 7 A, turn.
10th row: 7 A, 5 B, 2 A, 4 B, 8 A, turn.
11th –13th rows: 8 A, 10 B, 8 A, turn.
14th row: 7 A, 12 B, 7 A, turn.
15th row: 6 A, 15 B, 5 A, turn.
16th row: 4 A, 18 B, 4 A, turn.
17th row: 3 A, 21 B, 2 A, turn.
18th row: 2 A, 22 B, 2 A, turn.
19th row: 10 A, join on bobbin in B, 6 B, join on bobbin in A, 10 A.
20th row: 10 A, 5 B, 11 A, turn.
21st row: 11 A, 4 B, 11 A, turn.
22nd row: 11 A, 3 B, 12 A, turn.
23rd row: 12 A, 2 B, 12 A, turn.
24th row: 12 A, 1 B, 13 A, turn.
25th row: 13 A, 1 B, 12 A, turn.
26th row: As 24th.

27th–29th rows: With A only, work 3 rows in dc. Fasten off.

BACK:
Lower section:
With 2.50mm (UK 12) hook and A, make 26ch. Work foundation row as given for Front, then work 20 rows in dc.
Next row: Ss in each st to end. Fasten off.

Top flap:
With 2.50mm (UK 12) hook and A, make 26ch. Work foundation row as given for Front, then work 6 rows in dc.
Next row: 1ch (counts as first dc), miss first st, 1dc in each dc to last 2 sts, dc2tog over last 2 sts, turn.
1 st dec at end of row.
Rep last row until 18 sts rem.
Next row: Ss in each of first 5 sts, 7ch, miss next 7 sts, ss in each st to end. Fasten off.

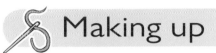 ## Making up

With WS facing, slip stitch front and back sections together around outer edges. Sew button to lower section of back to correspond with chain loop.
Cushion pad:
With RS facing, sew around outer edges of cotton squares, taking 5mm seam allowances and leaving a small gap for turning through. Turn RS out and stuff firmly with polyester toy filling. Neatly slip stitch opening closed. Insert pad into cover and button closed.

Classic turban

Turban-style hats are back in vogue; this stylish example features straightforward stitches.

Worked in 4-ply yarn and rows of ridged half trebles with a knotted band, this stylish headwear has retro appeal.

The Yarn
Debbie Bliss Rialto 4-Ply (approx. 180m/ 196 yards per 50g/1¾oz ball) is 100% Merino wool in a machine-washable format. It produces a soft fabric and there is a wide colour range.

GETTING STARTED

★ ★ *Worked mainly in half trebles with a double crochet knot.*

Size:
To fit an average-sized woman's head

How much yarn:
2 x 50g (1¾oz) balls Debbie Bliss Rialto 4-ply in teal (shade 018)

Hook:
3.50mm (UK 9) crochet hook

Tension:
23 sts and 18 rows measure 10cm (4in) square over patt on 3.50mm (UK 9) hook
IT IS ESSENTIAL TO WORK TO THE STATED TENSION TO ACHIEVE SUCCESS

What you have to do:
Work main band and crown in half trebles working into back loop of each stitch. Work knot in double crochet. Join short ends of main band then wrap knot around seam. Sew crown in position.

Instructions

Abbreviations:

beg = beginning
ch = chain
cm = centimetre(s)
cont = continue
dc = double crochet
htr = half treble
htr2tog = (yrh, insert hook in next st and draw loop through) twice, yrh and draw through all 5 loops
inc = increased
patt = pattern
rep = repeat
RS = right side
sp = space
st(s) = stitch(es)
WS = wrong side
yrh = yarn round hook

TURBAN:
Main band:

With 3.50mm (UK 9) hook make 122ch.
Foundation row: (WS) 1htr into 3rd ch from hook, 1htr into each ch to end, turn. 120htr.
Patt row: 2ch (does not count as a st), 1htr into back loop only of each htr to end, turn.
Rep patt row until work measures 12cm (4¾in) from beg, ending with a RS row. Fasten off.

Crown:

With 3.50mm (UK 9) hook make 30ch. Work foundation row as given for main band. 28htr.
Next row: 2ch, working into back loop only of each st, work 2htr into first htr, 1htr into each htr to last htr, 2htr into last htr, turn. 1 st inc at each end.
Patt 1 row as given for main band.
Rep last 2 rows 3 times more. 36 sts.
Cont straight in patt until crown measures 14cm (5½in) from beg.
Last row: 2ch, (htr2tog) to end. 18 sts. Fasten off.

Knot:

With 3.50mm (UK 9) hook make 10ch.
Foundation row: 1dc into 2nd ch from

hook, I dc into each ch to end, turn. 9dc.

Next row: I ch (does not count as a st), I dc into each dc to end, turn. Rep last row until work measures 11cm (4¼in) from beg. Fasten off.

✄ Making up

Using a long length of yarn, join short ends of main band, then work a row of running sts along seam. Pull end of yarn to gather seam, but do not fasten off. With RS of main band facing, wrap knot around gathered seam and join ends of knot on WS. Sew end of running thread securely on WS. Work a few small sts on WS of main band to hold knot securely in position. With WS facing, pin centre of foundation row of crown to centre of top of knot, and centre of last row of crown to top edge of main band at centre back. Pin crown in place evenly around main band. Join with a backstitch seam.

Index

Acknowledgements

Managing Editor: Clare Churly
Editors: Lesley Malkin and Eleanor van Zandt
Senior Art Editor: Juliette Norsworthy
Designer: Janis Utton
Production Controller: Allison Gonsalves